Magic Garden In a Jar

Adult Coloring Book

BRUSH MAGIC

Color Testing Page

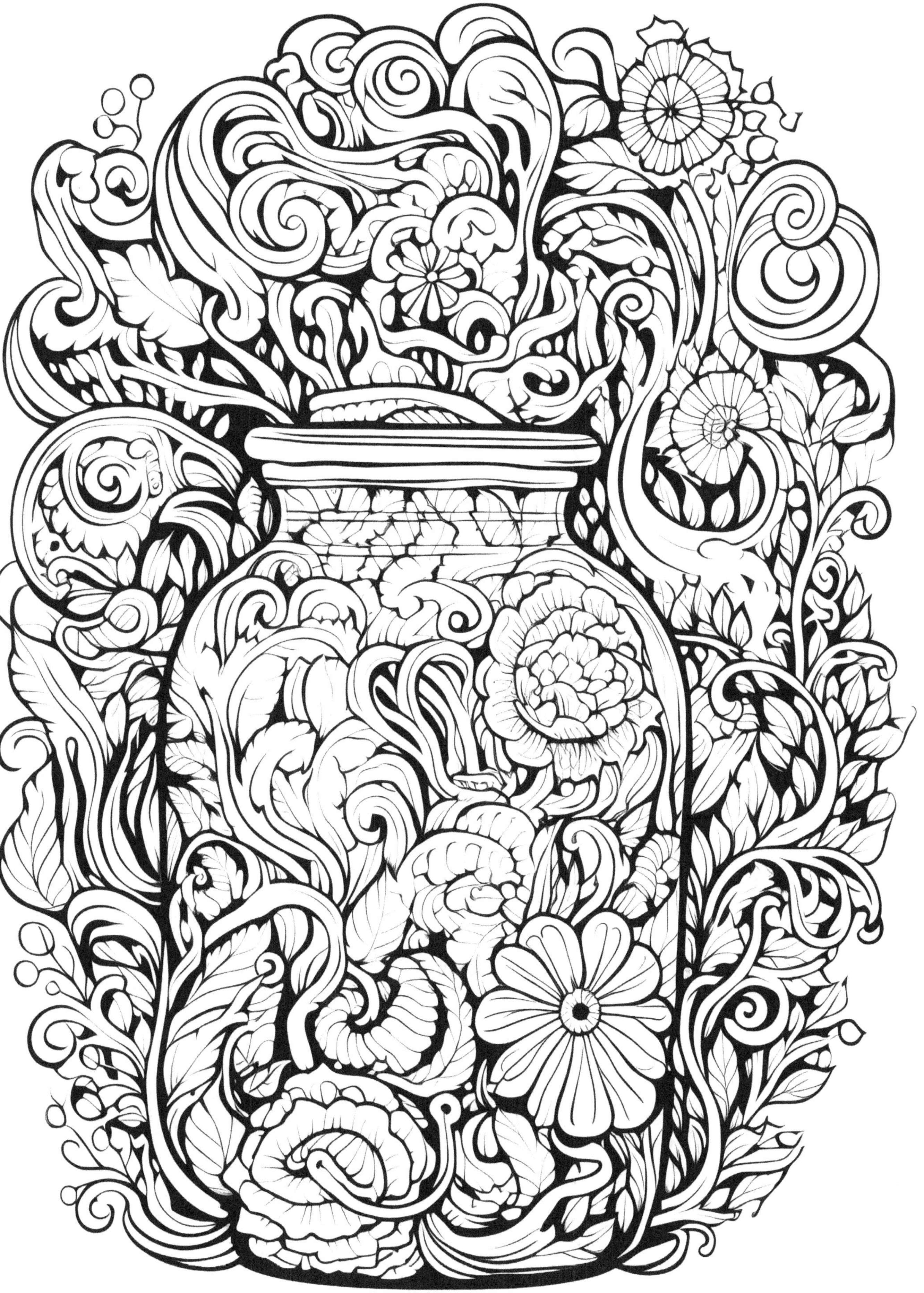

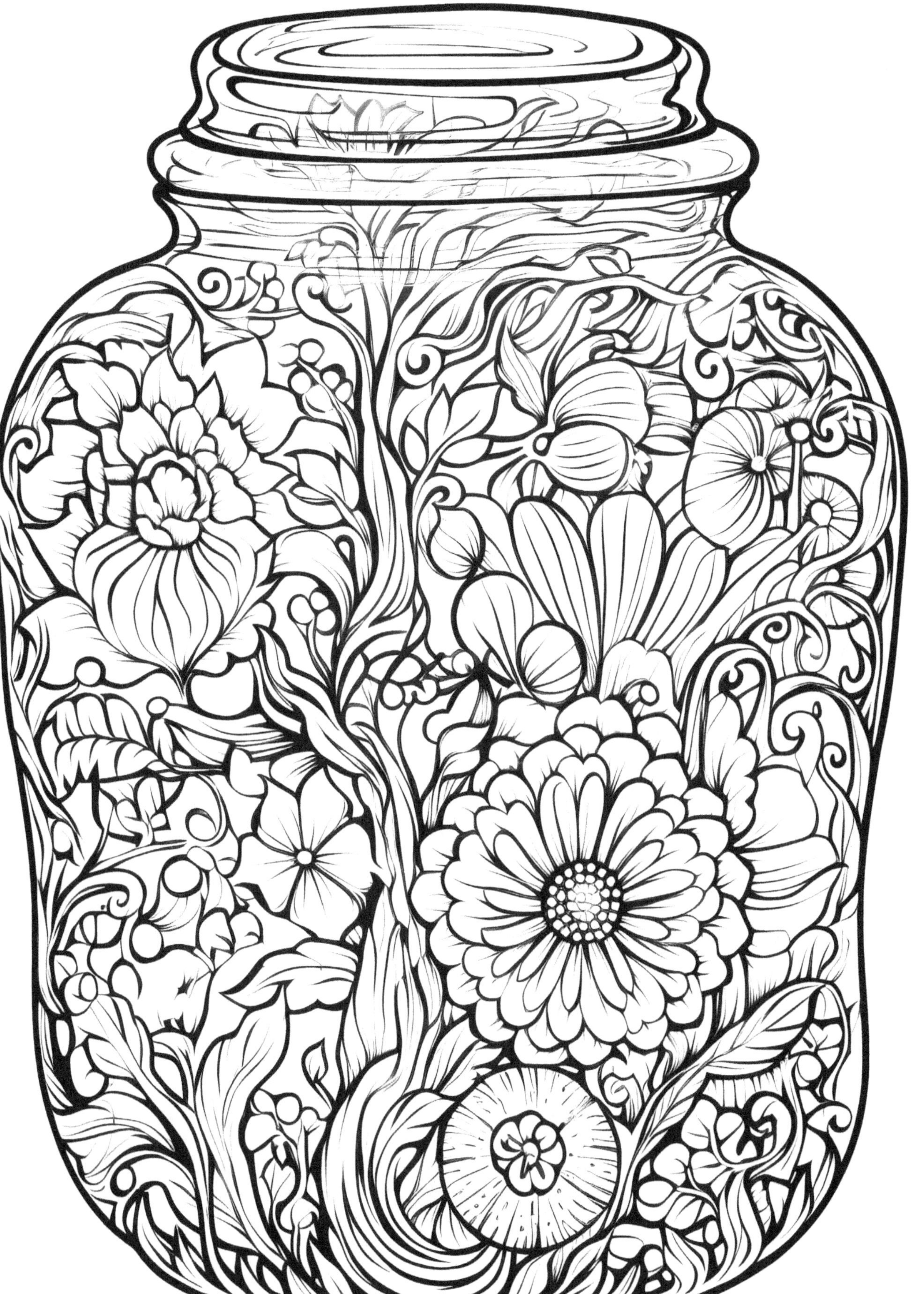

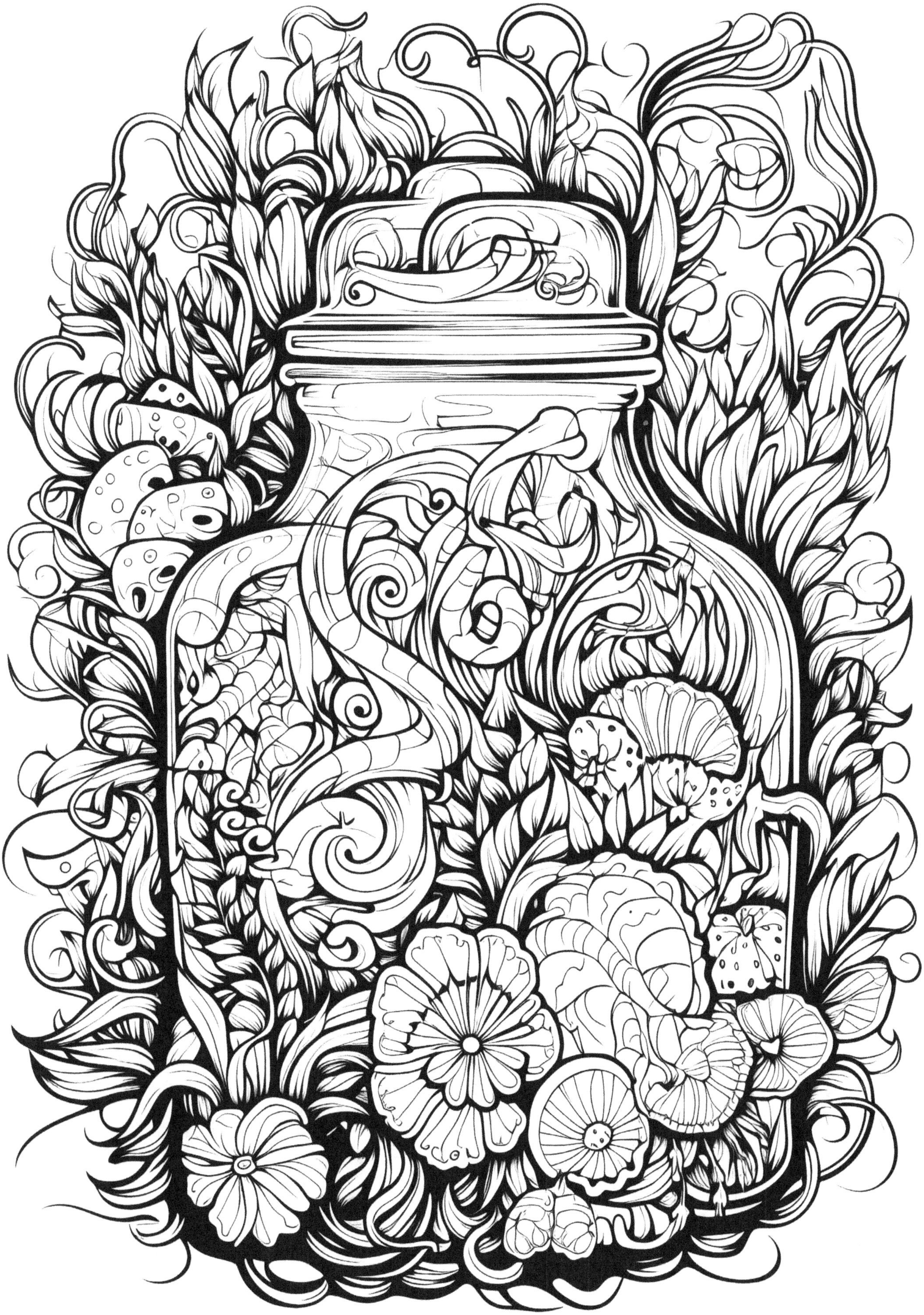

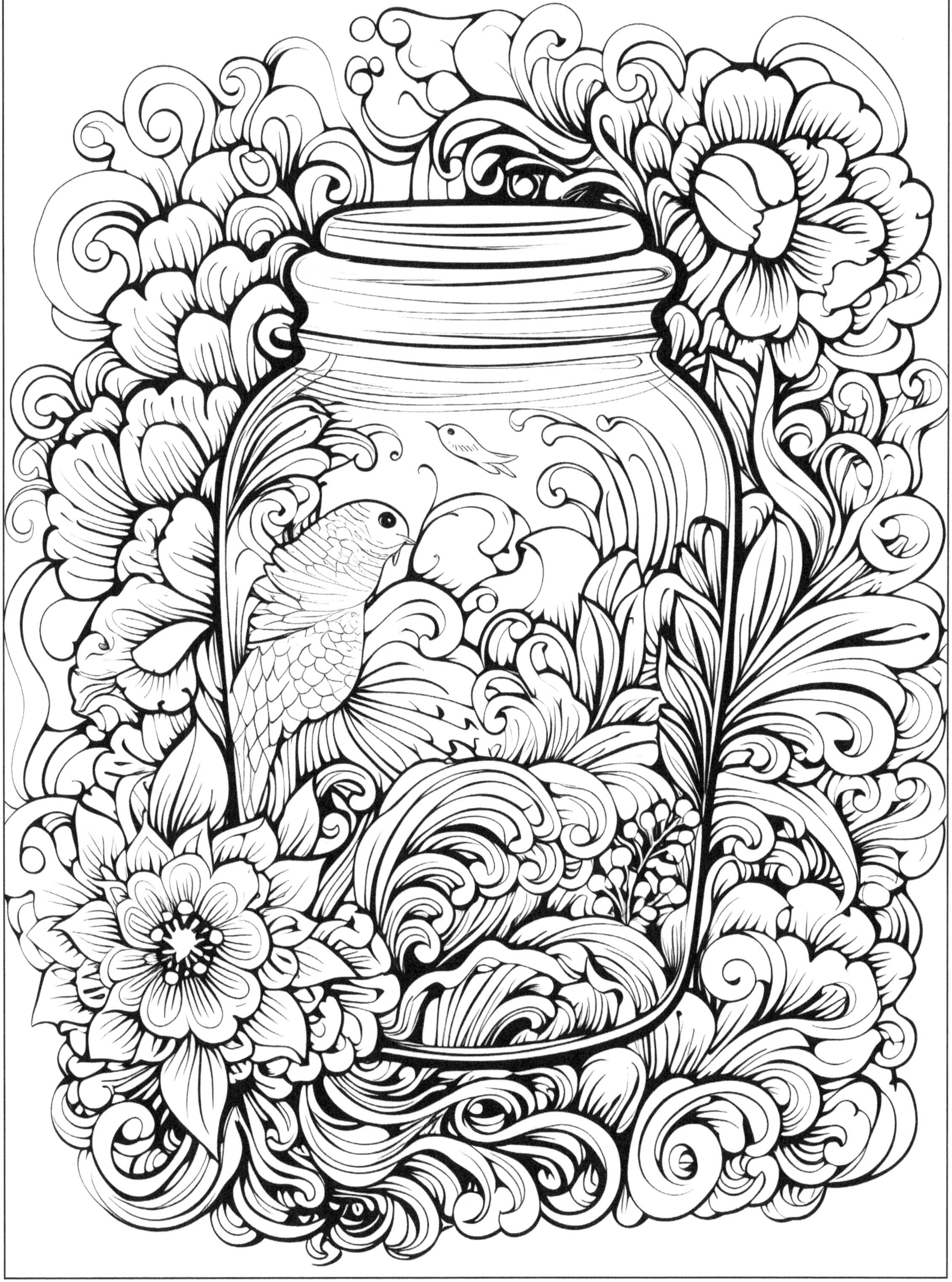

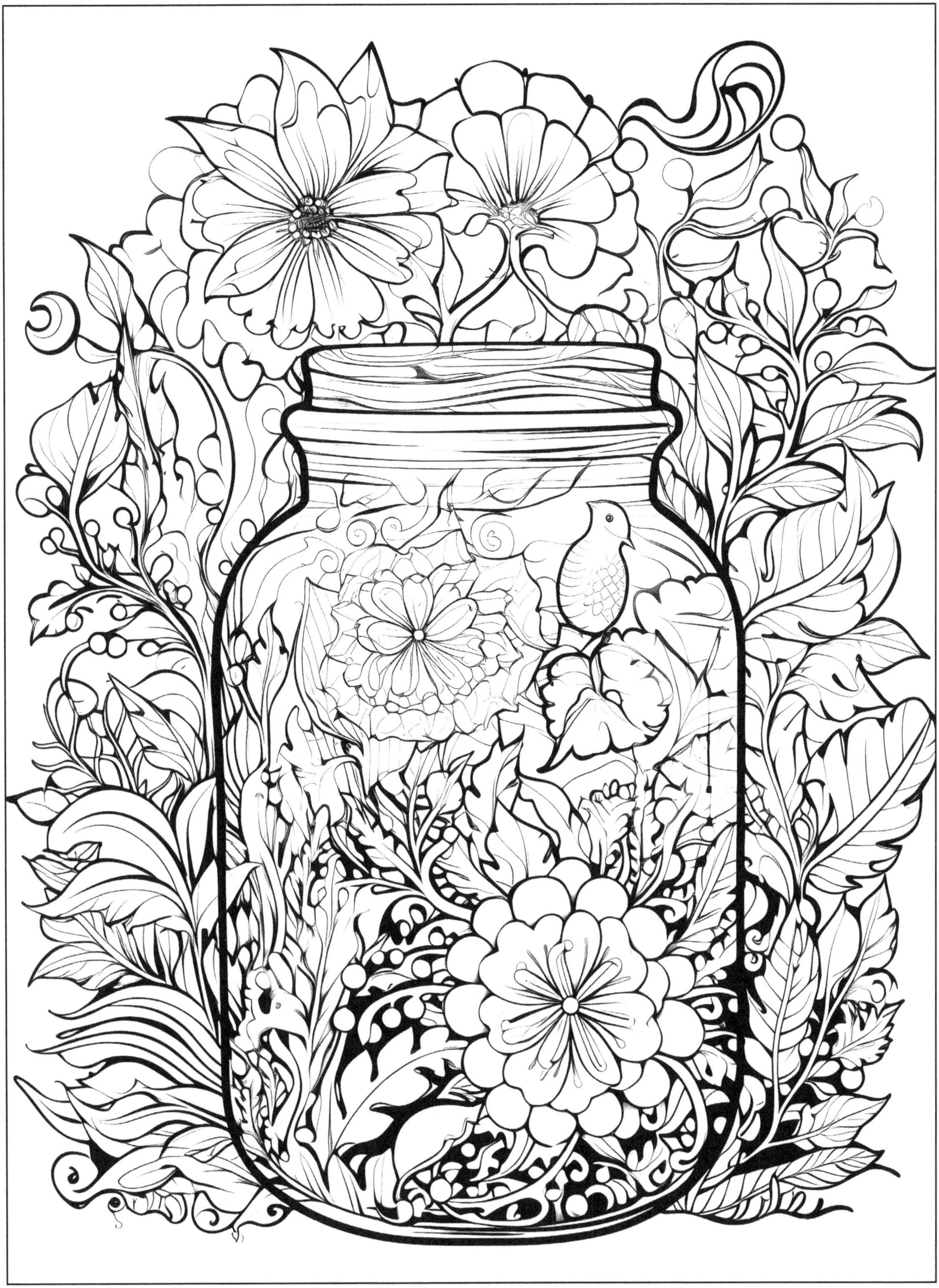

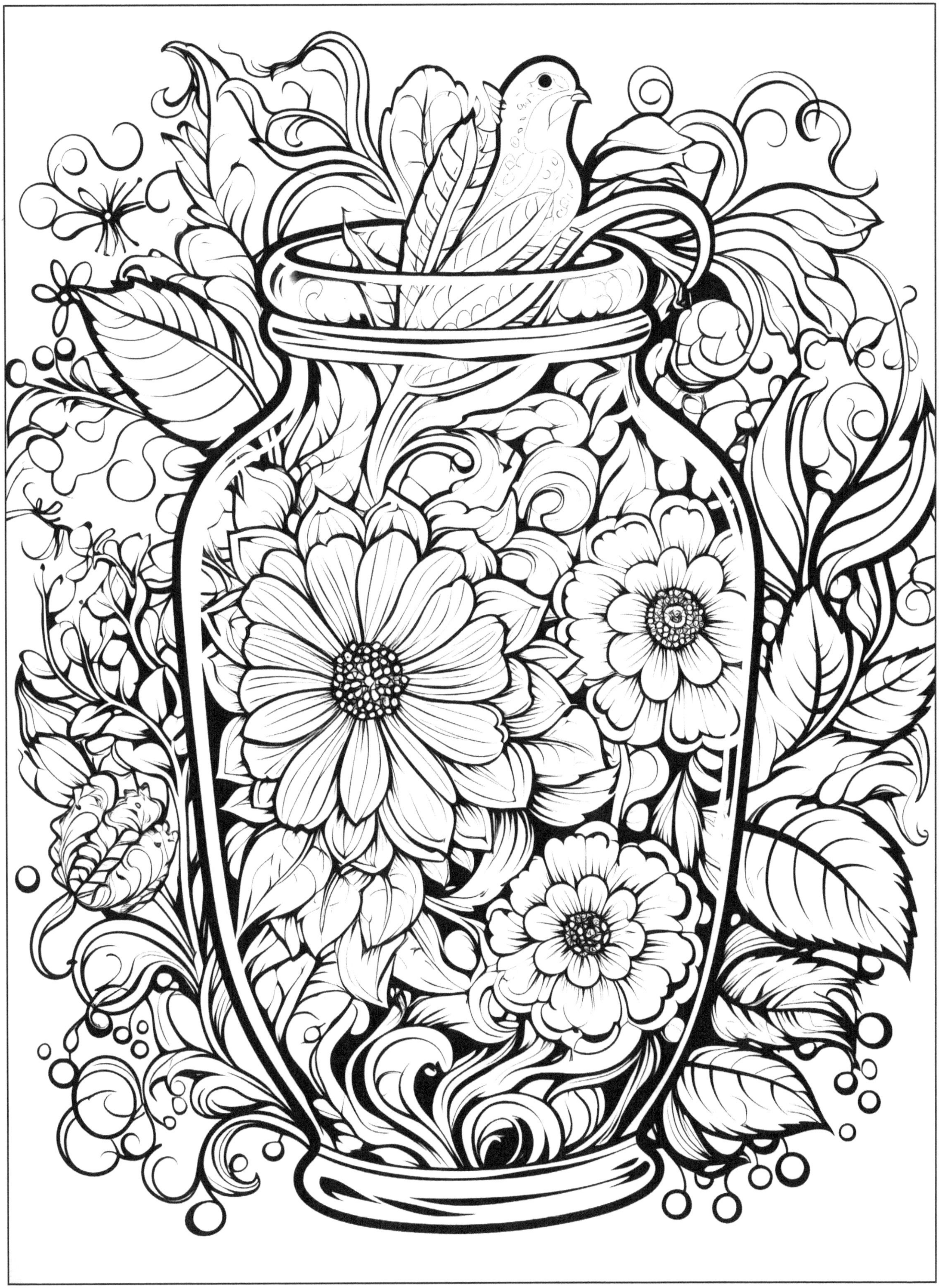

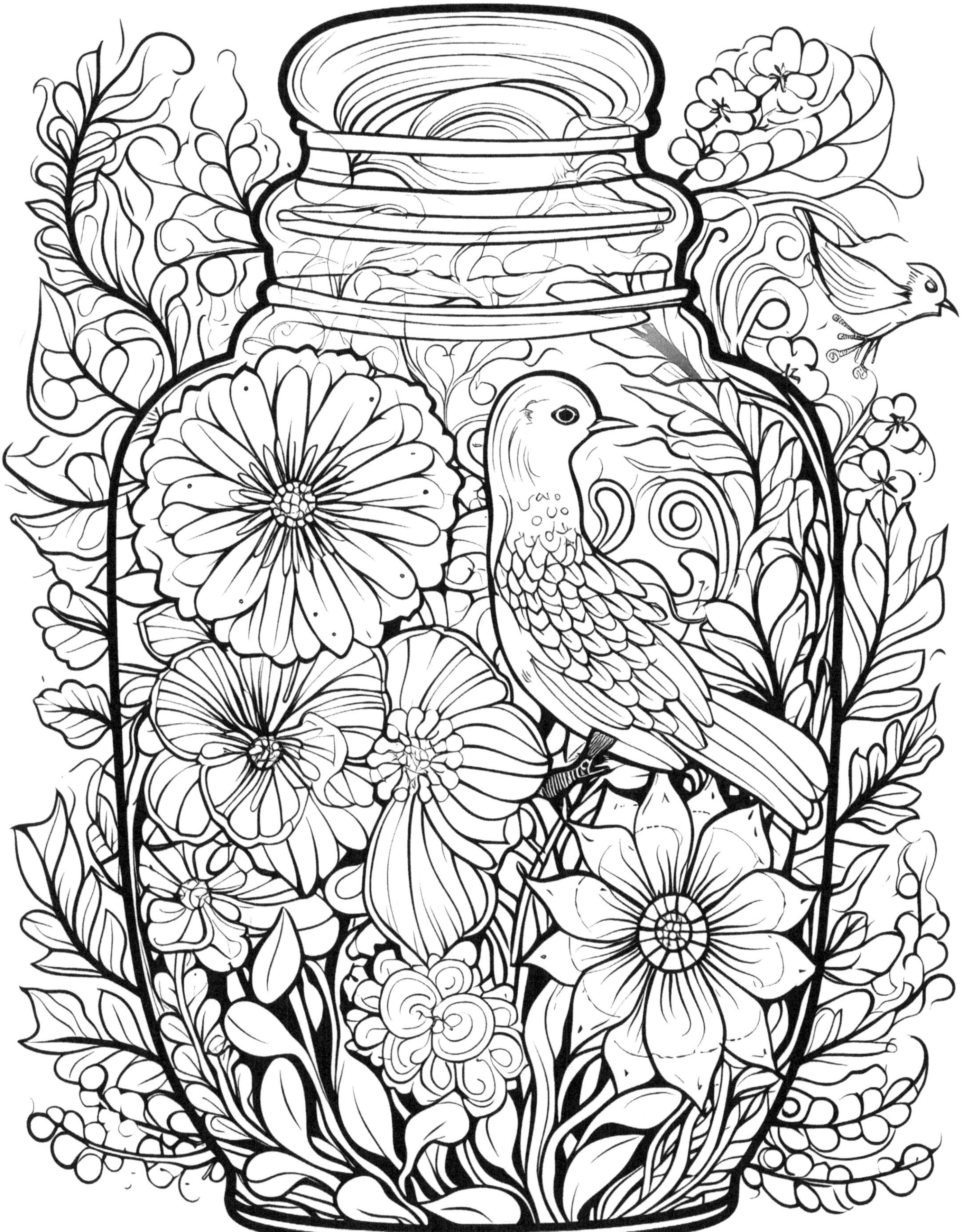

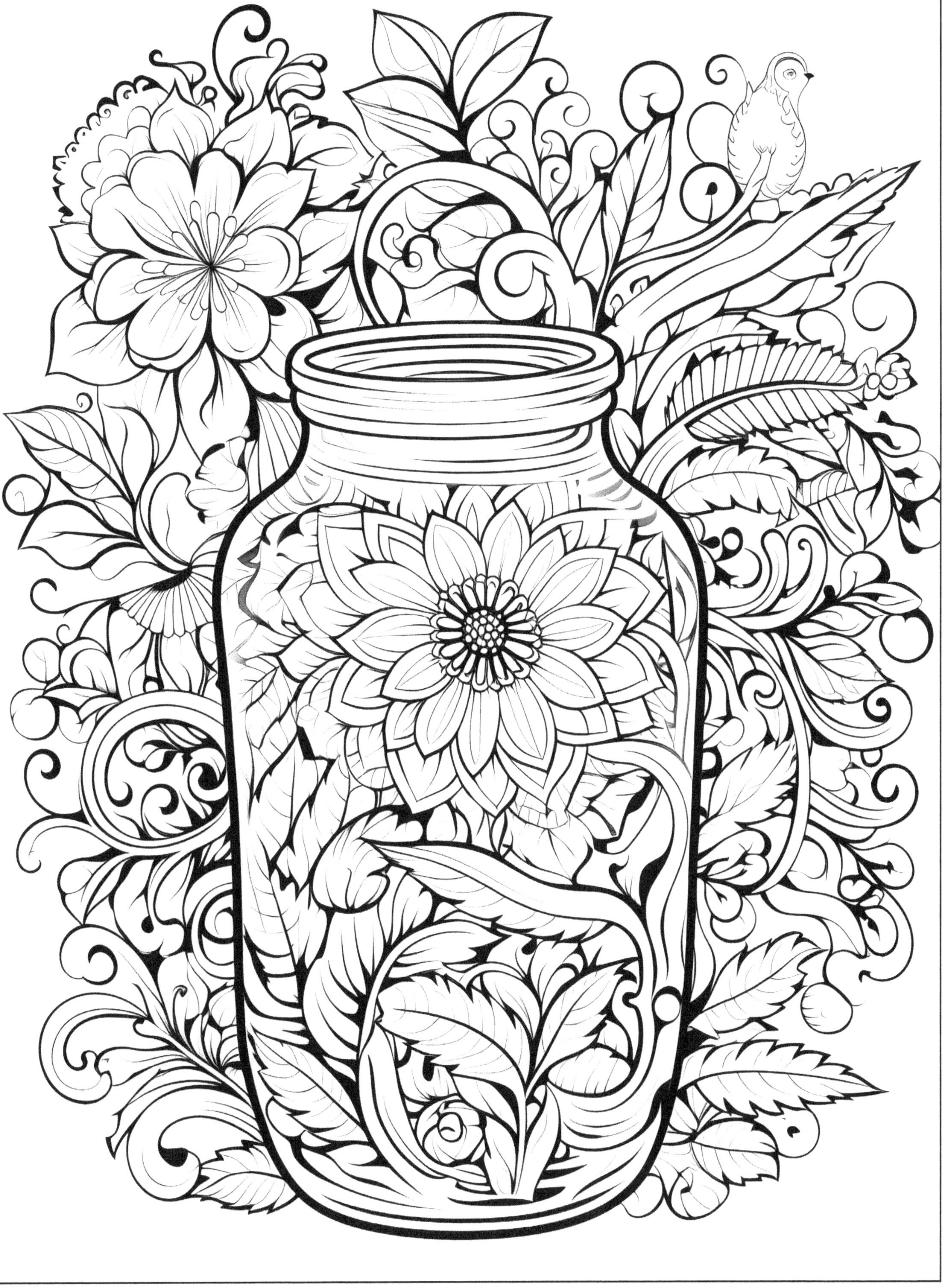

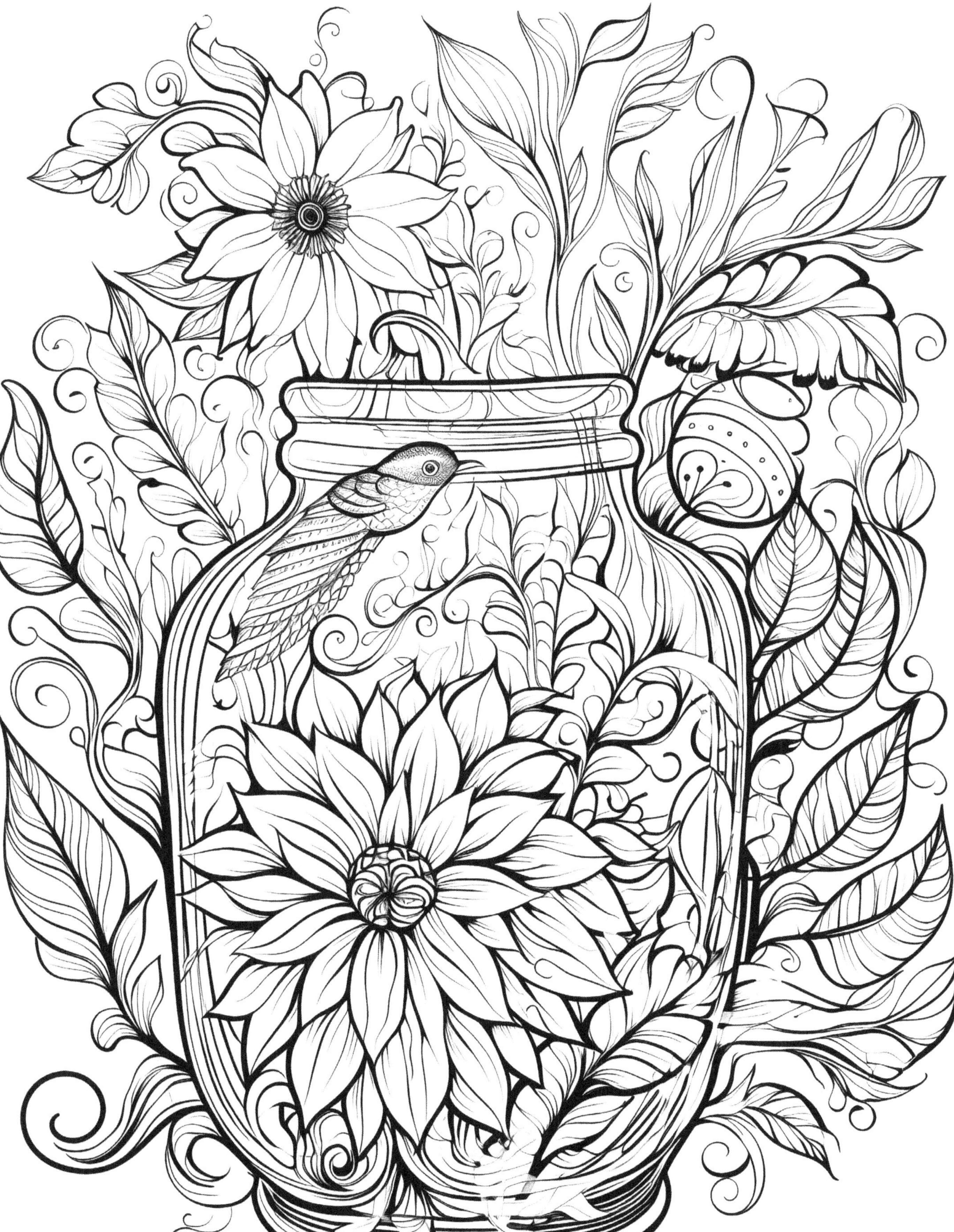

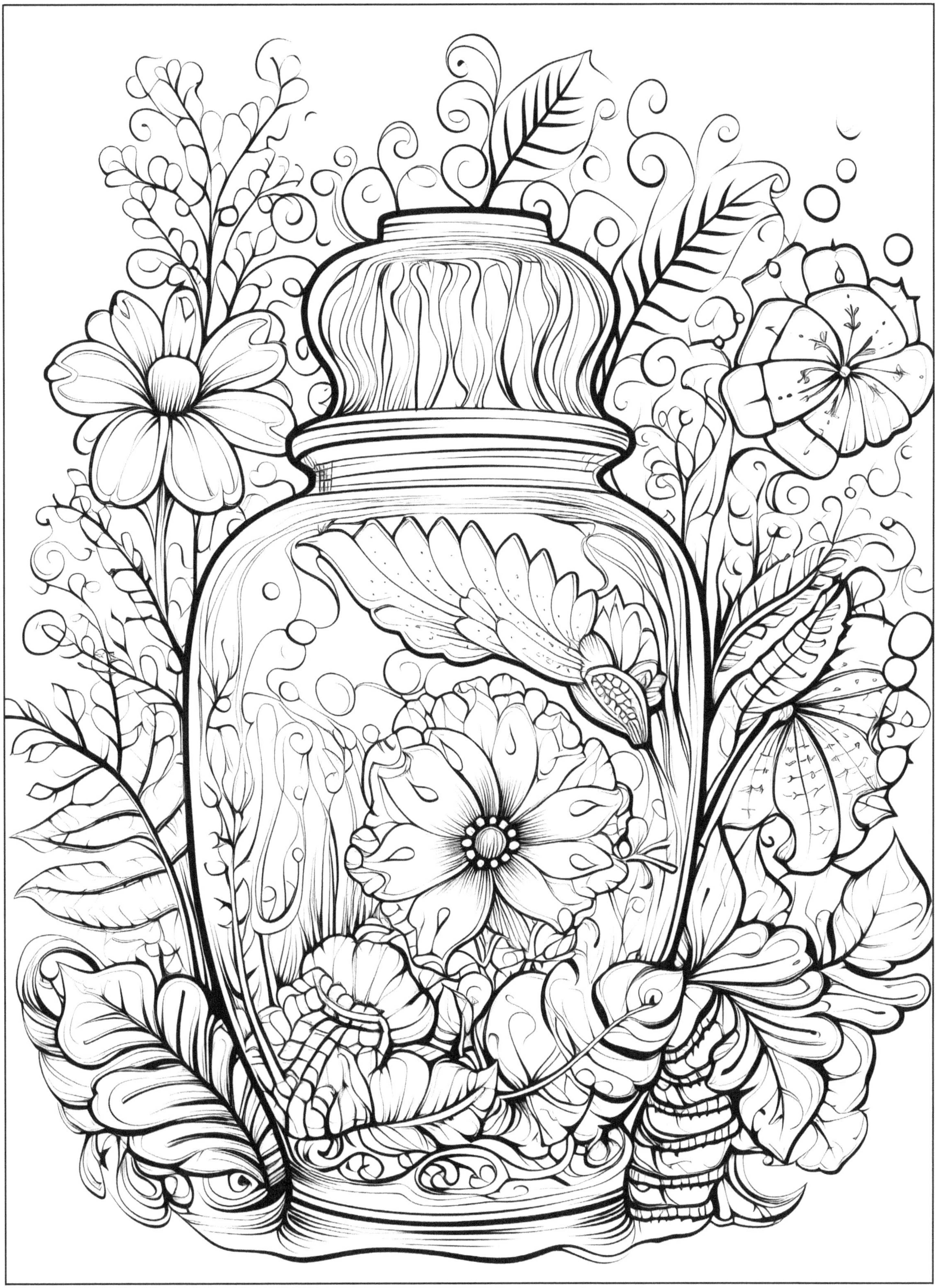

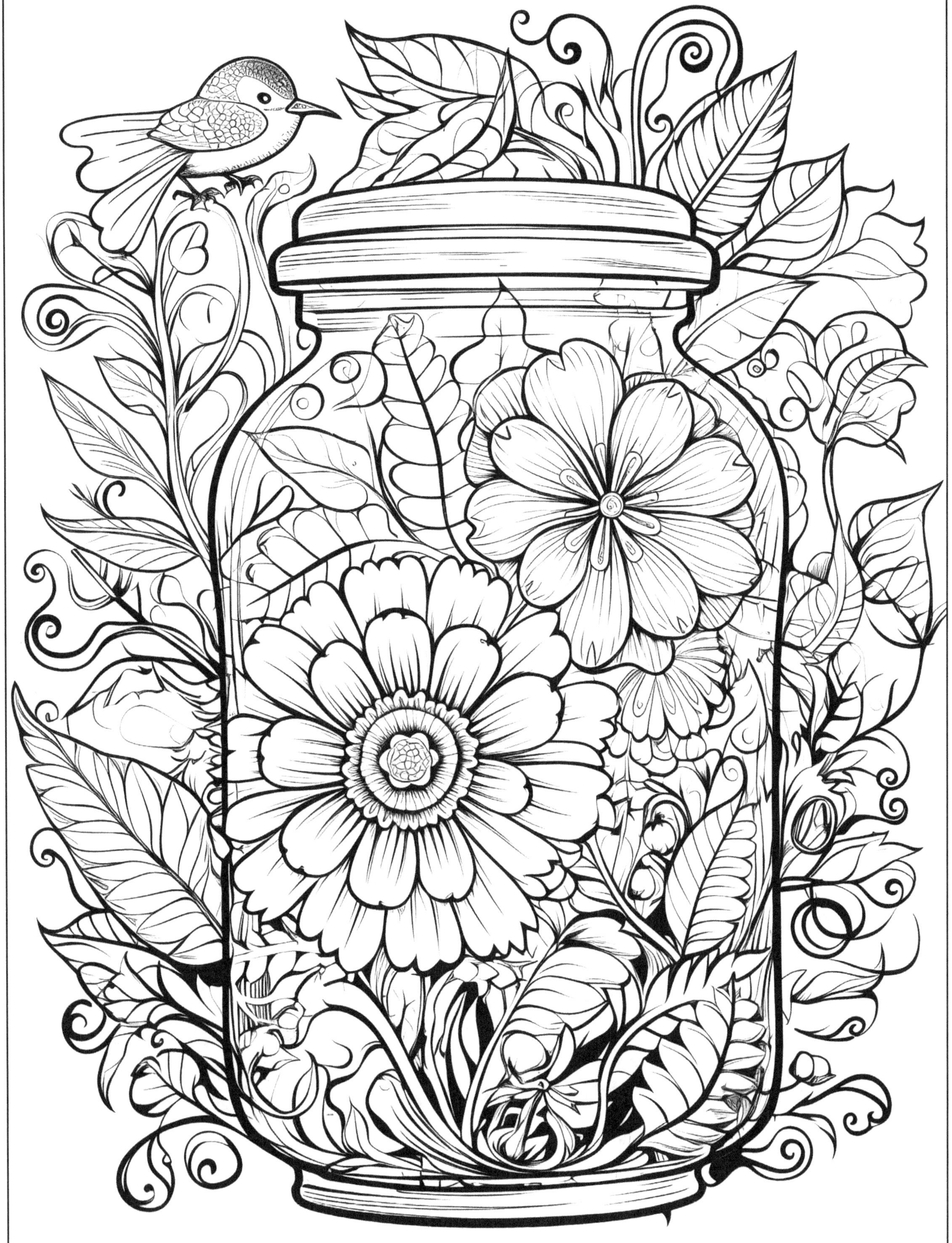

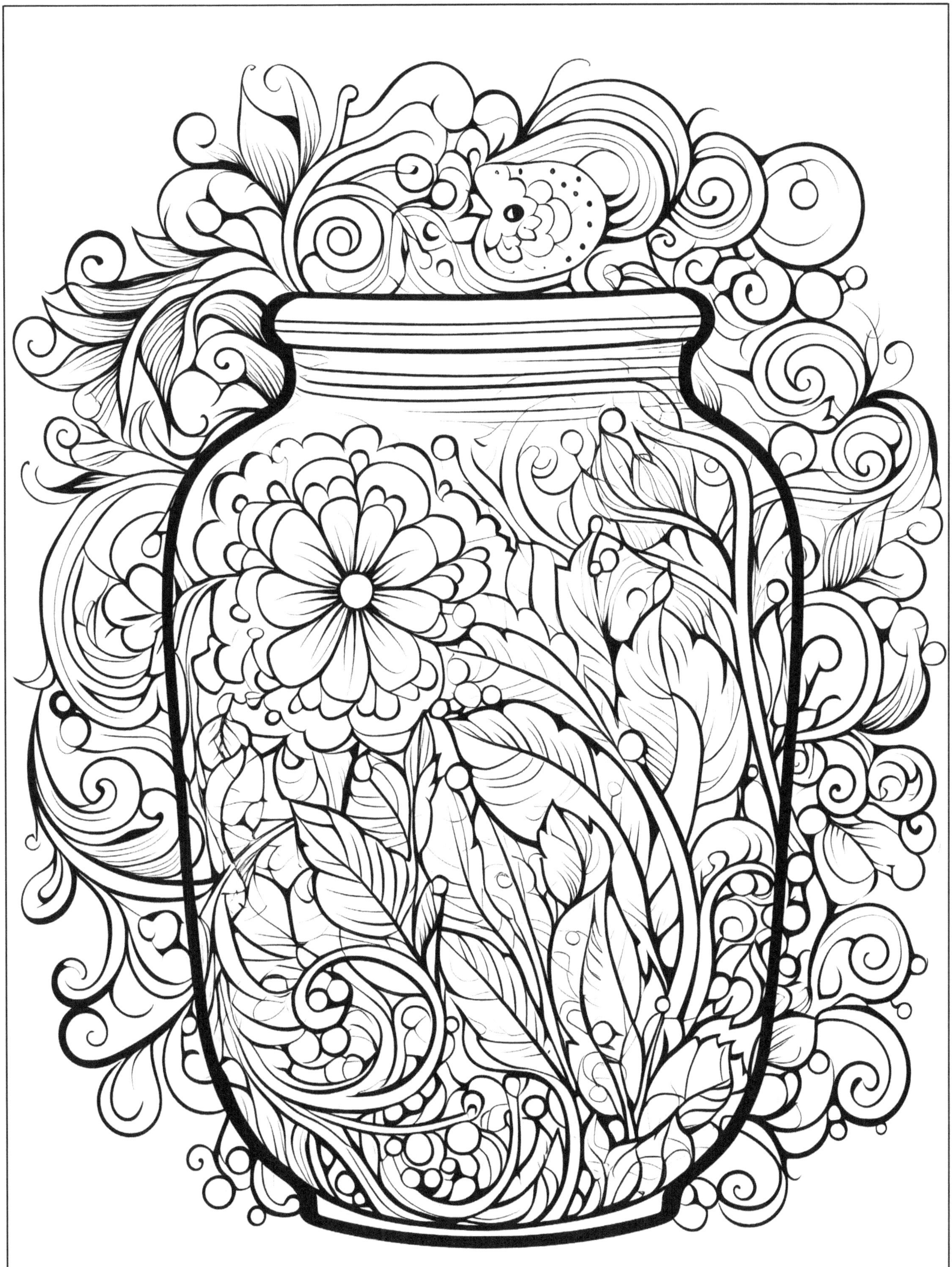

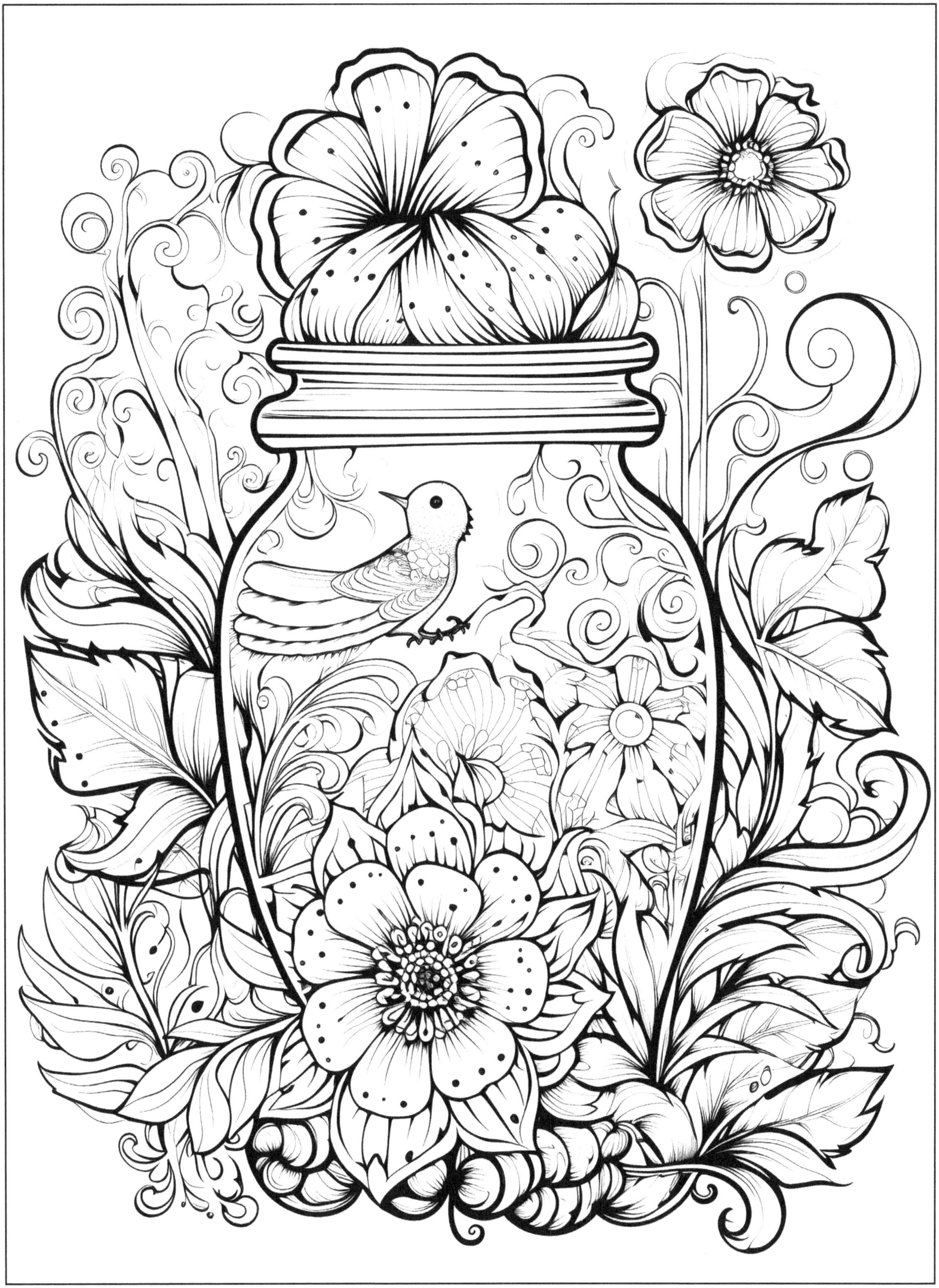

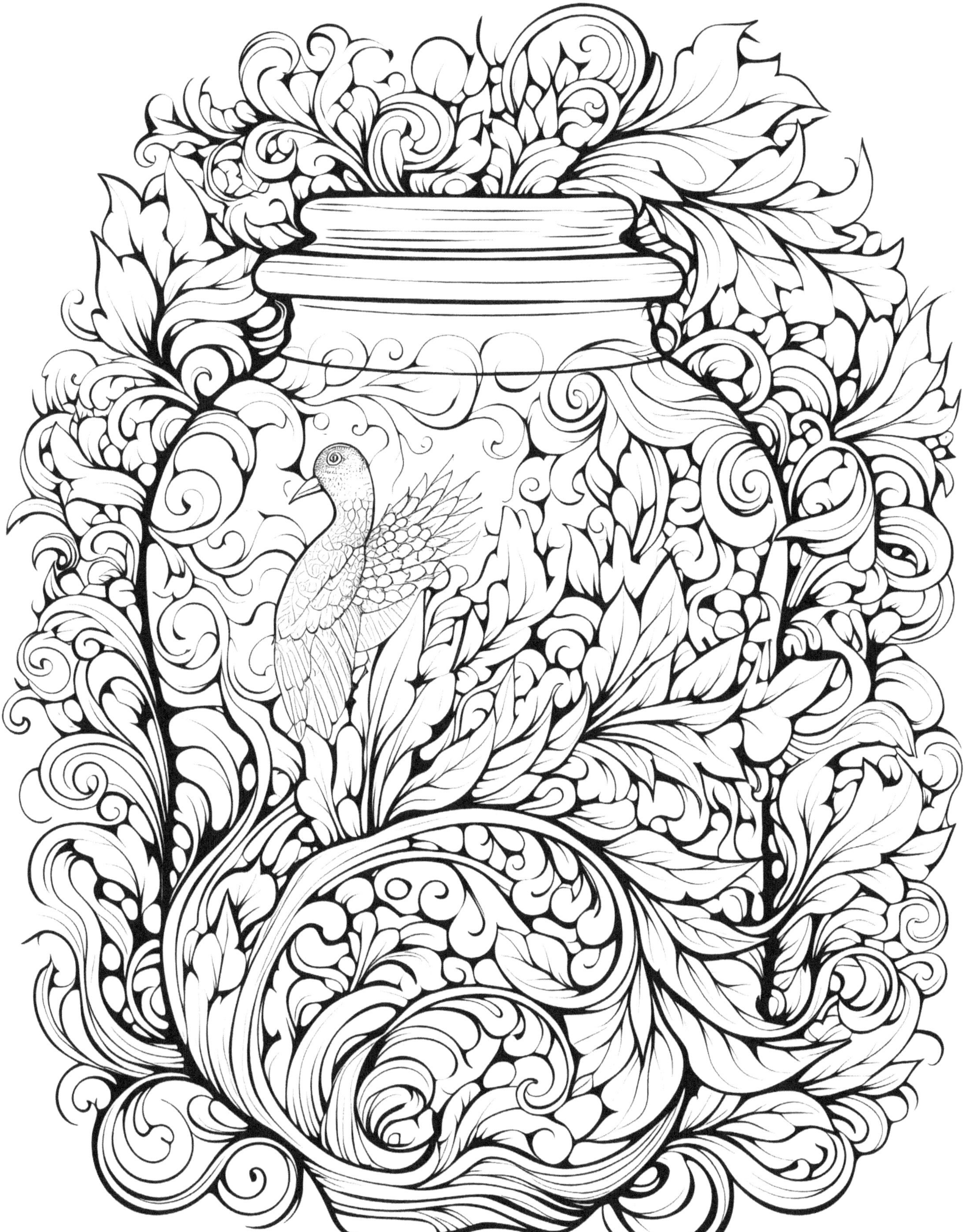

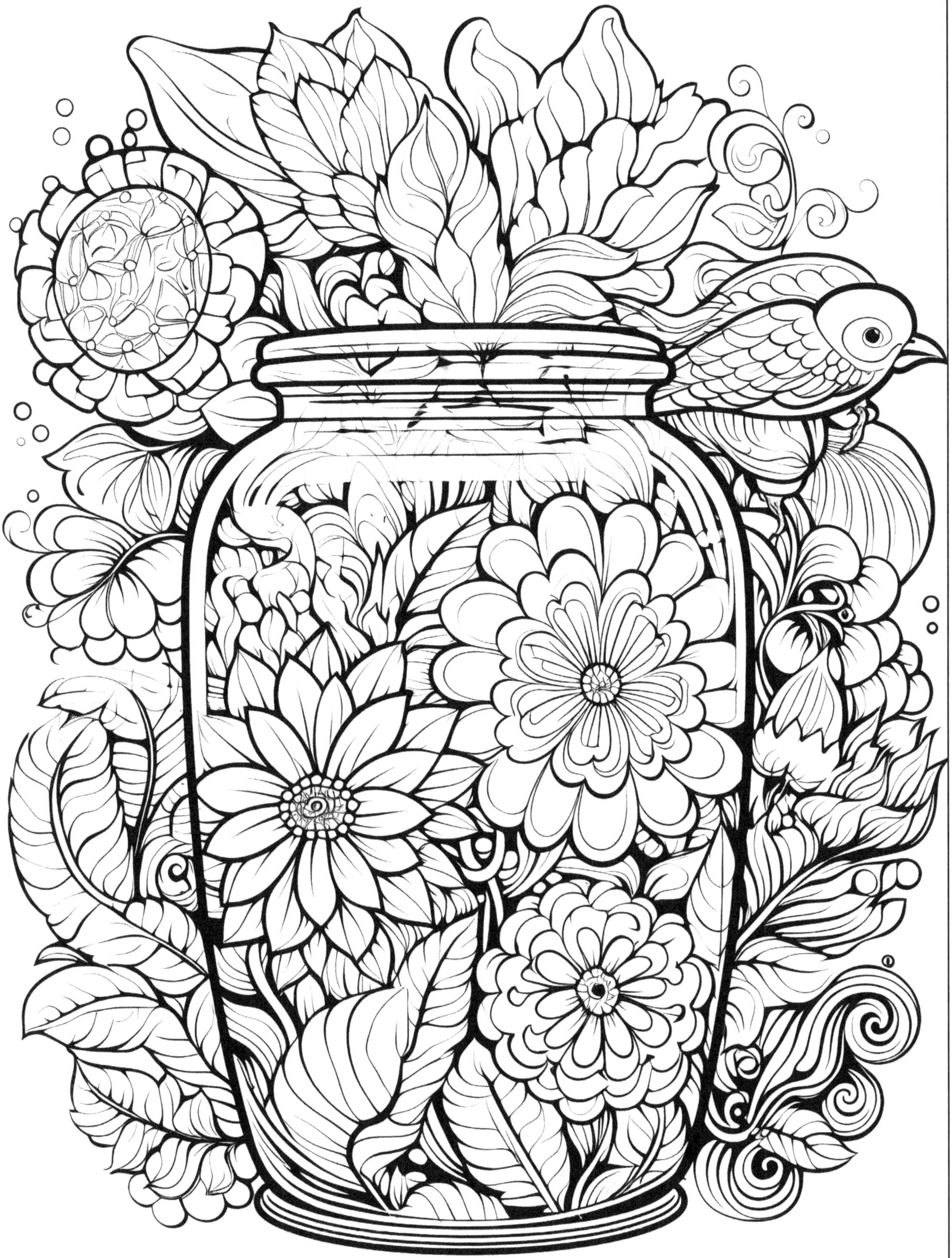

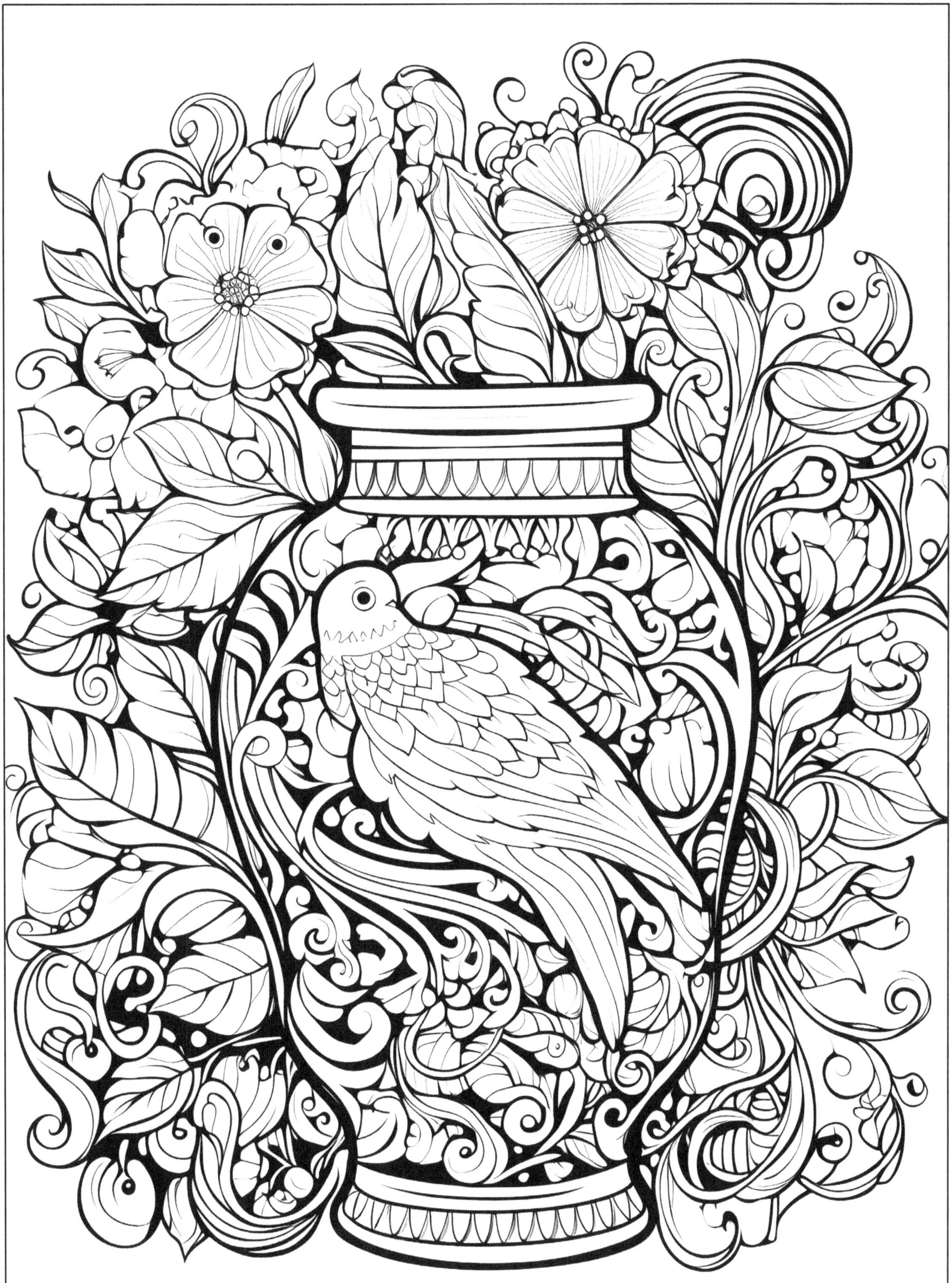

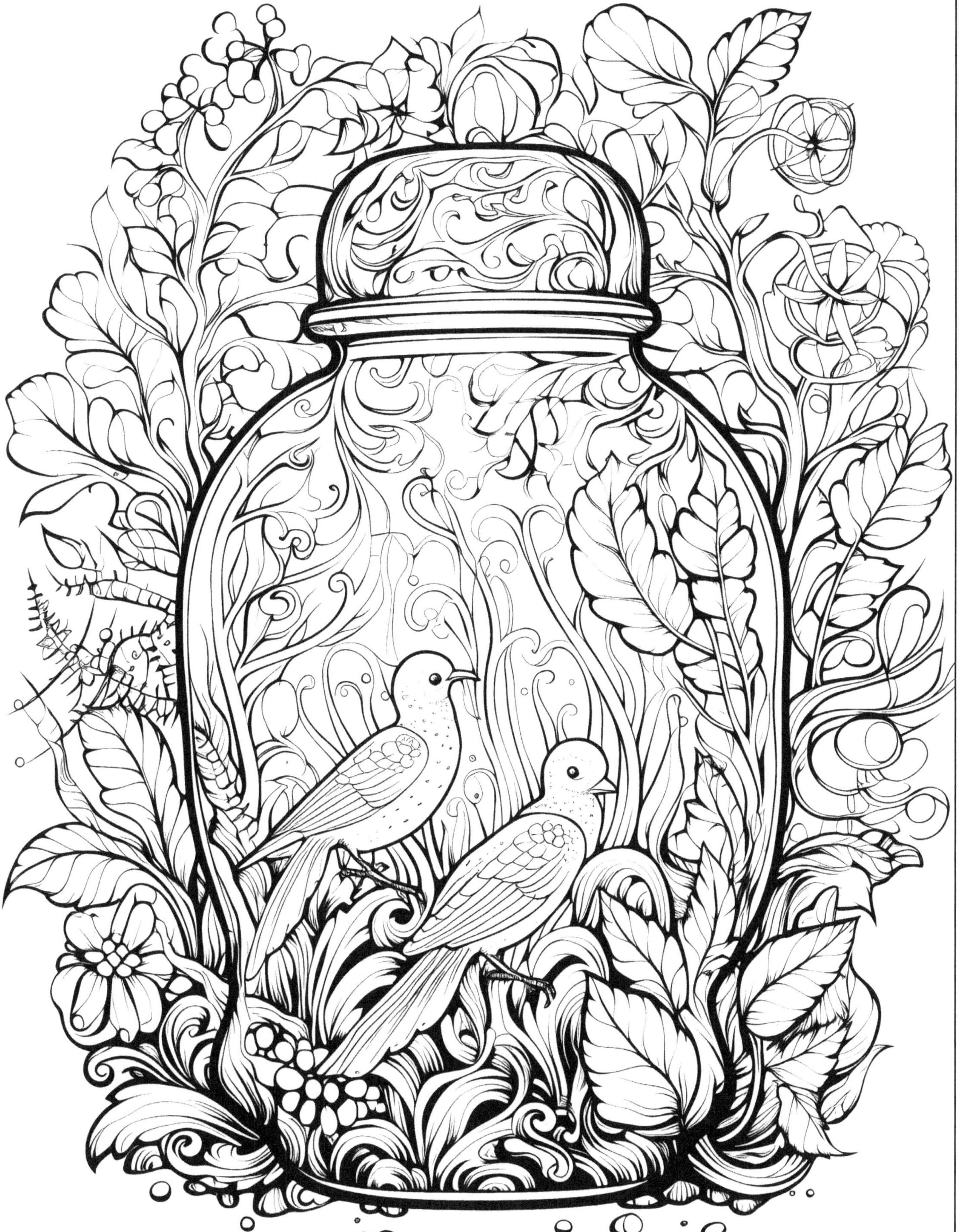

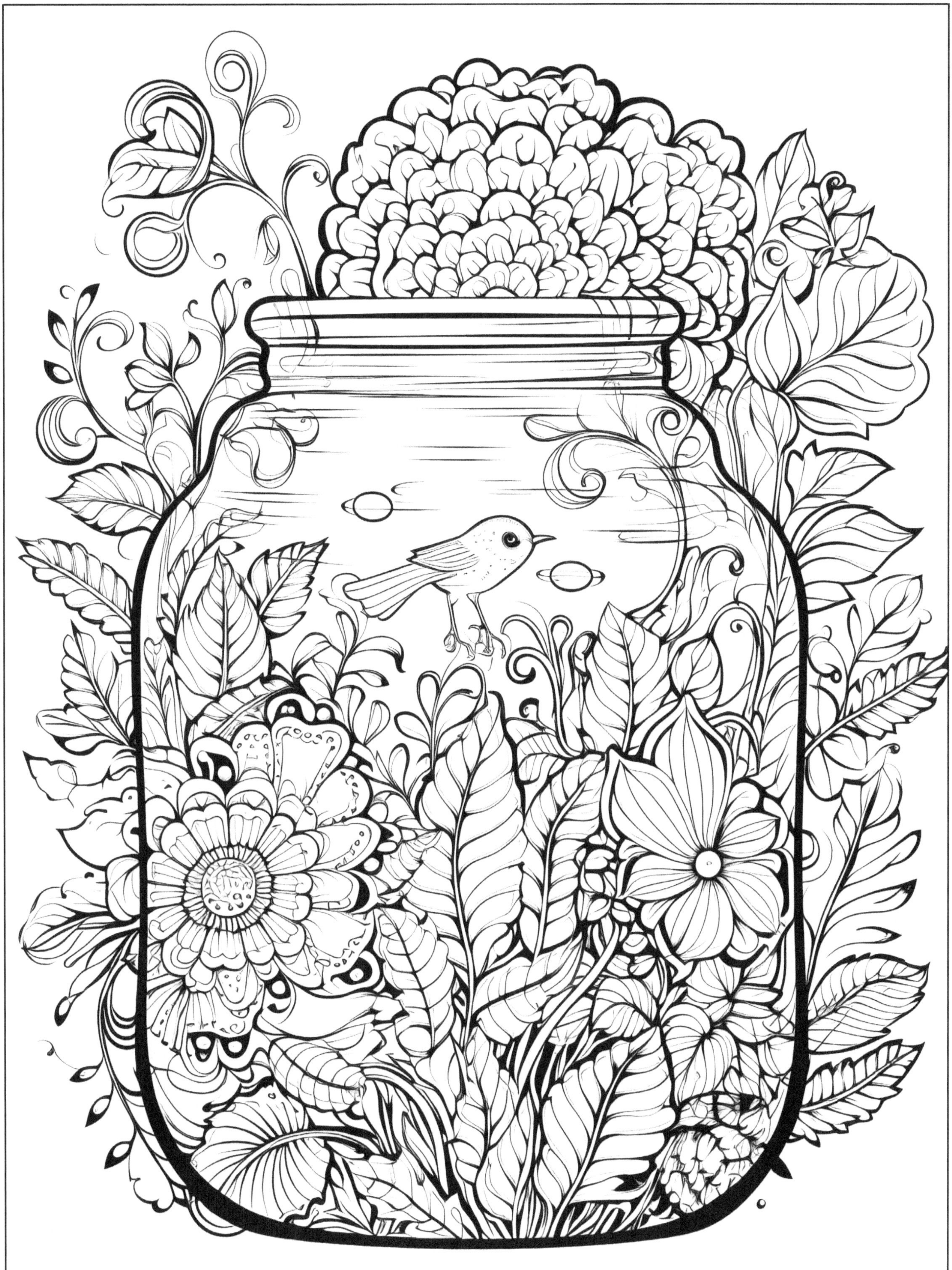

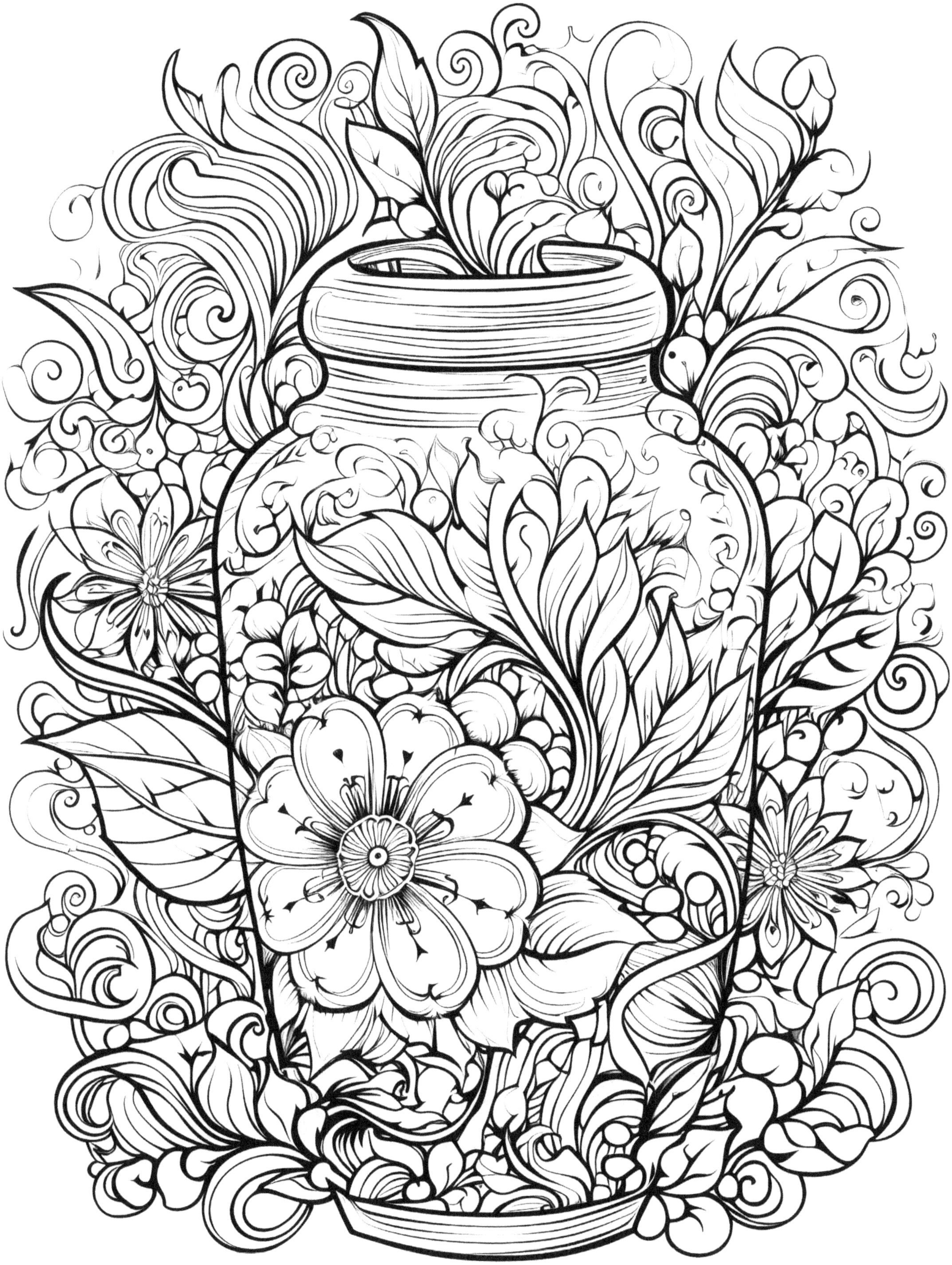

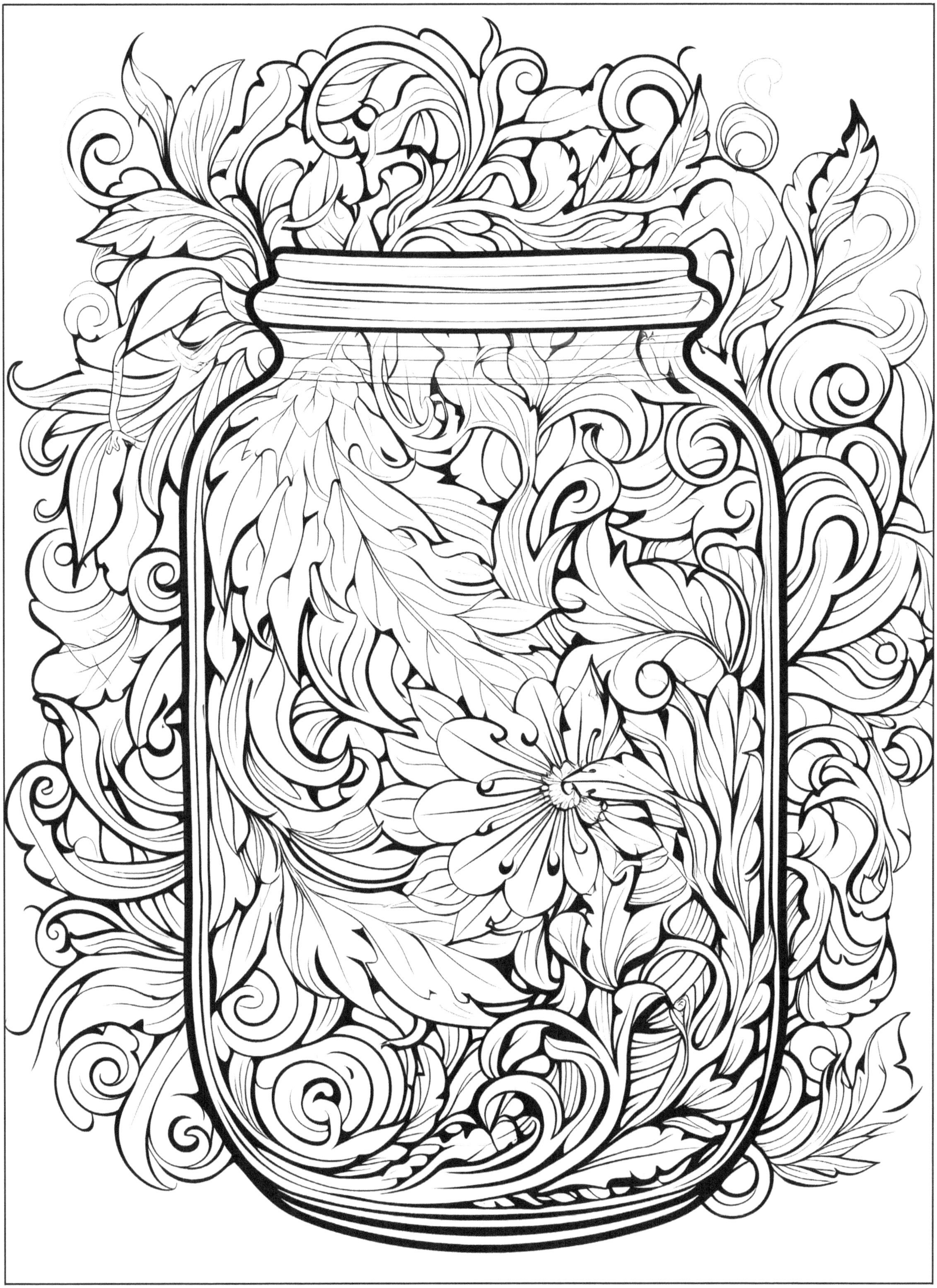

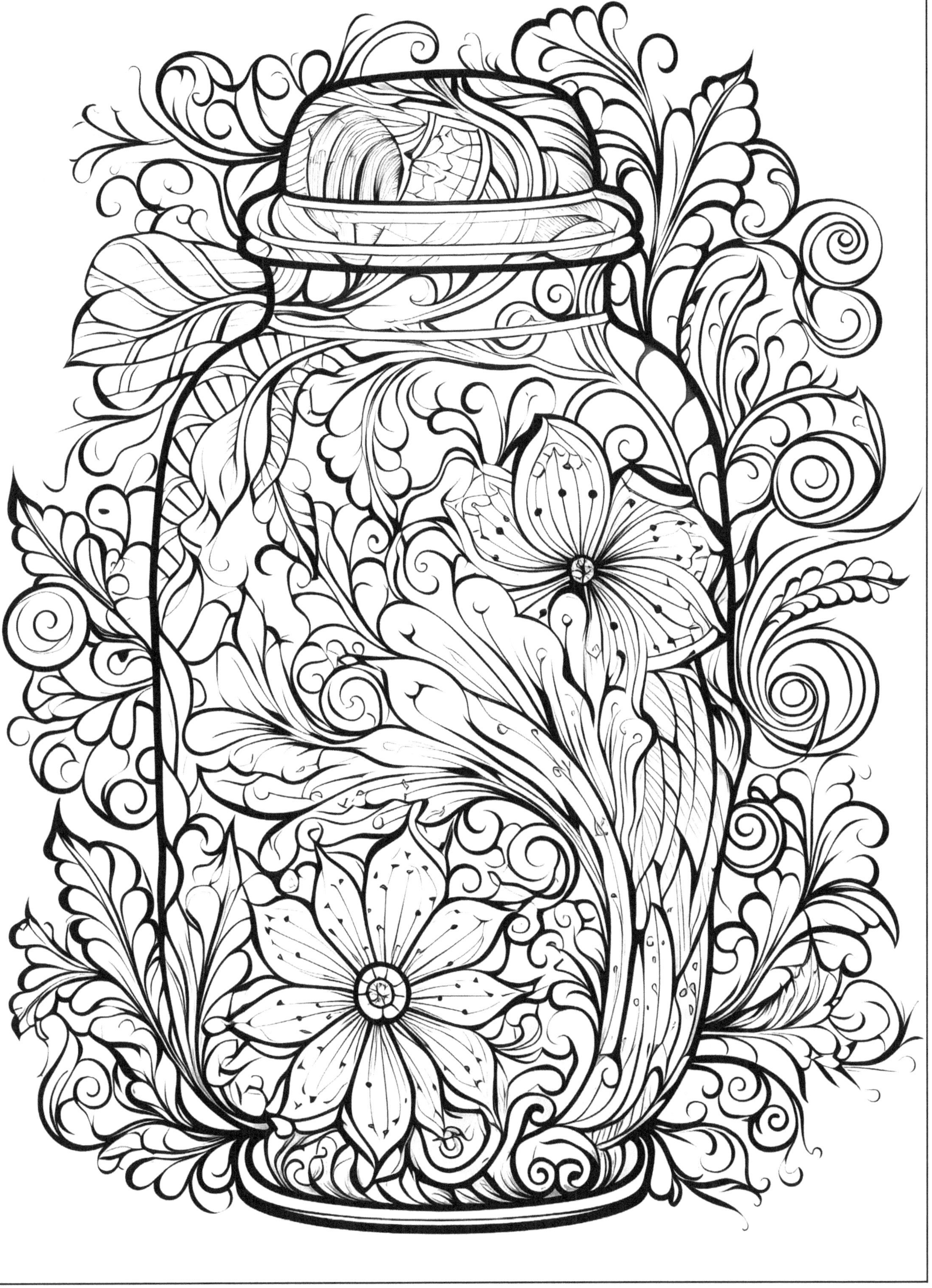

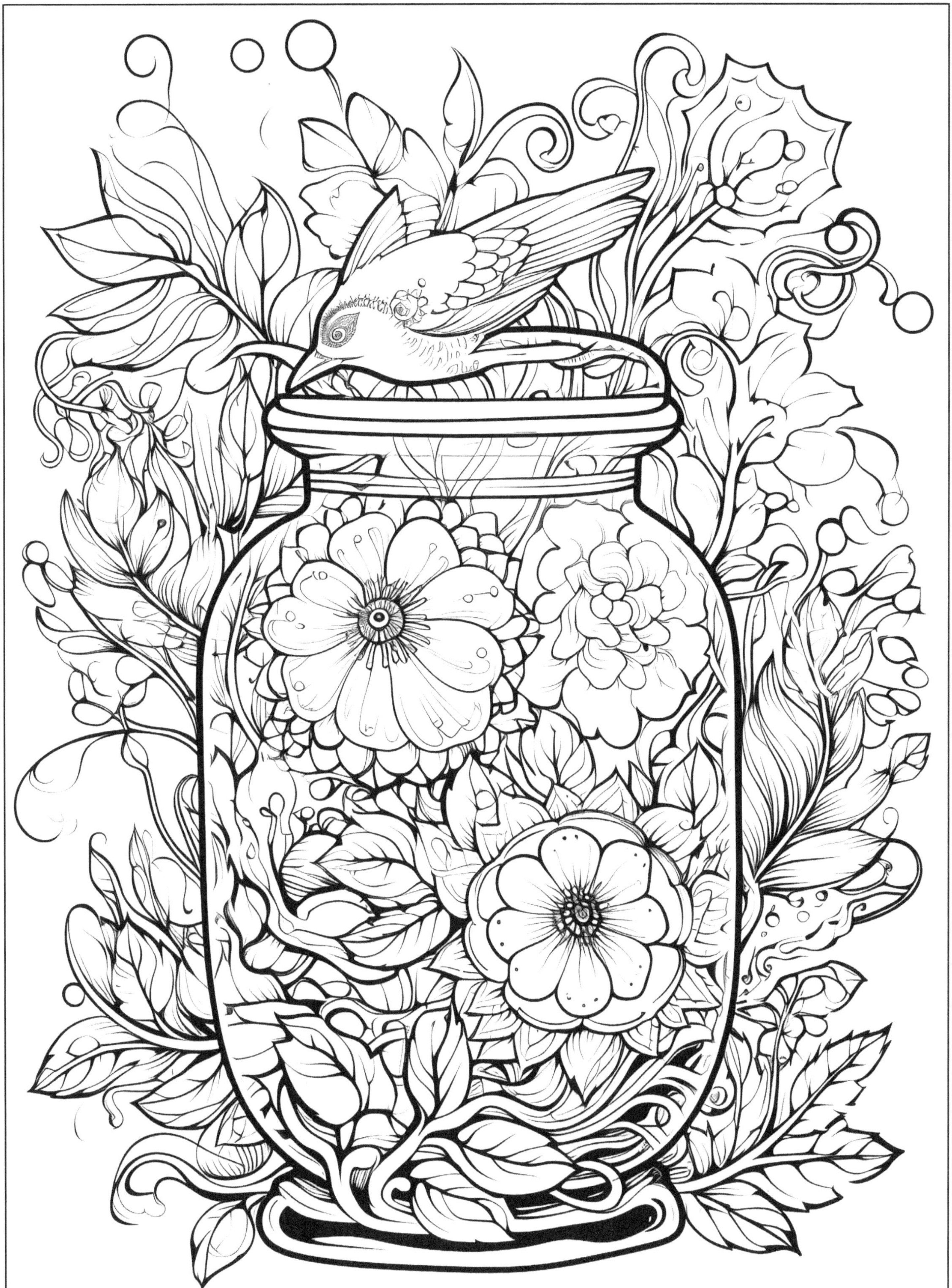

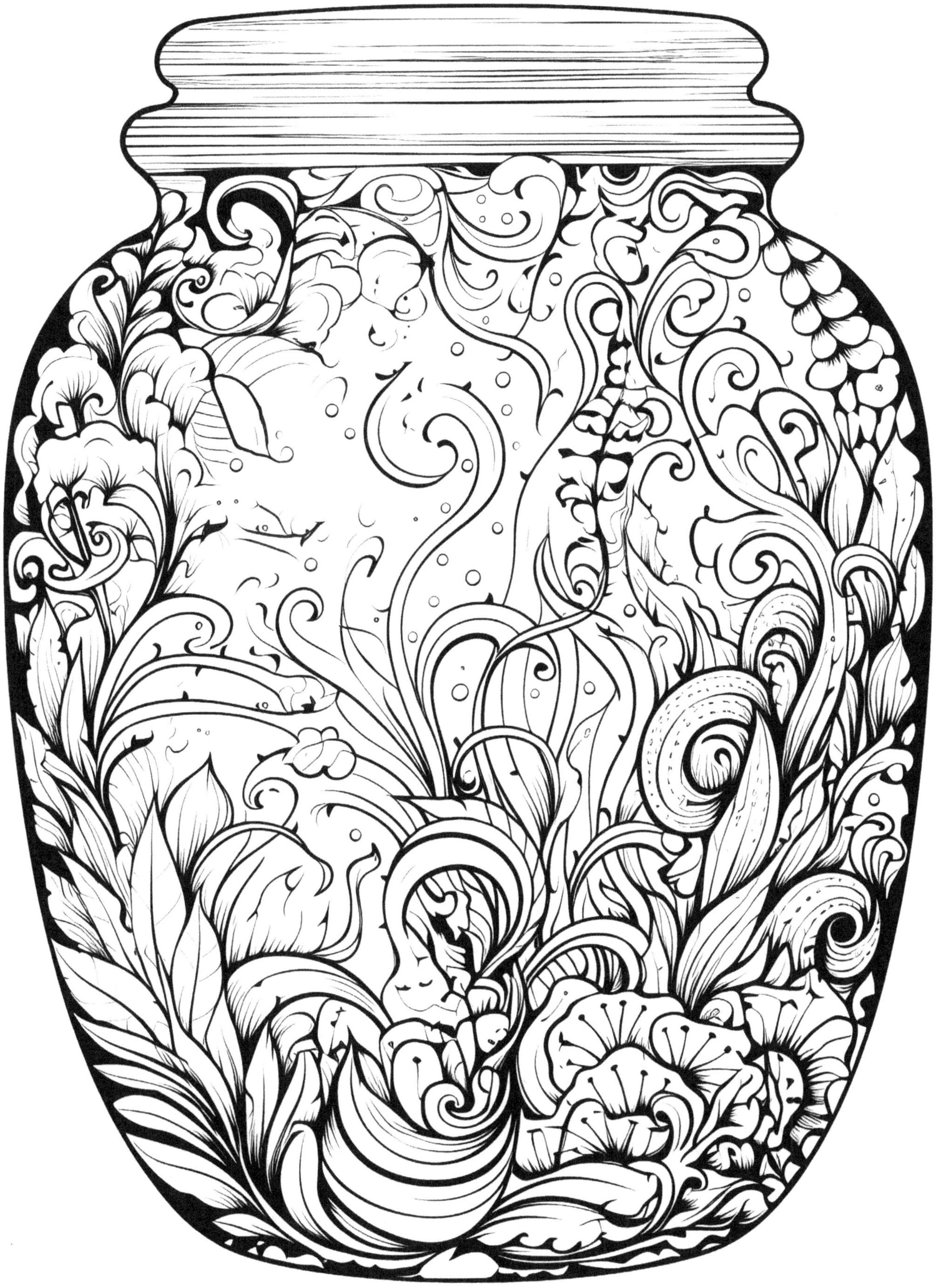

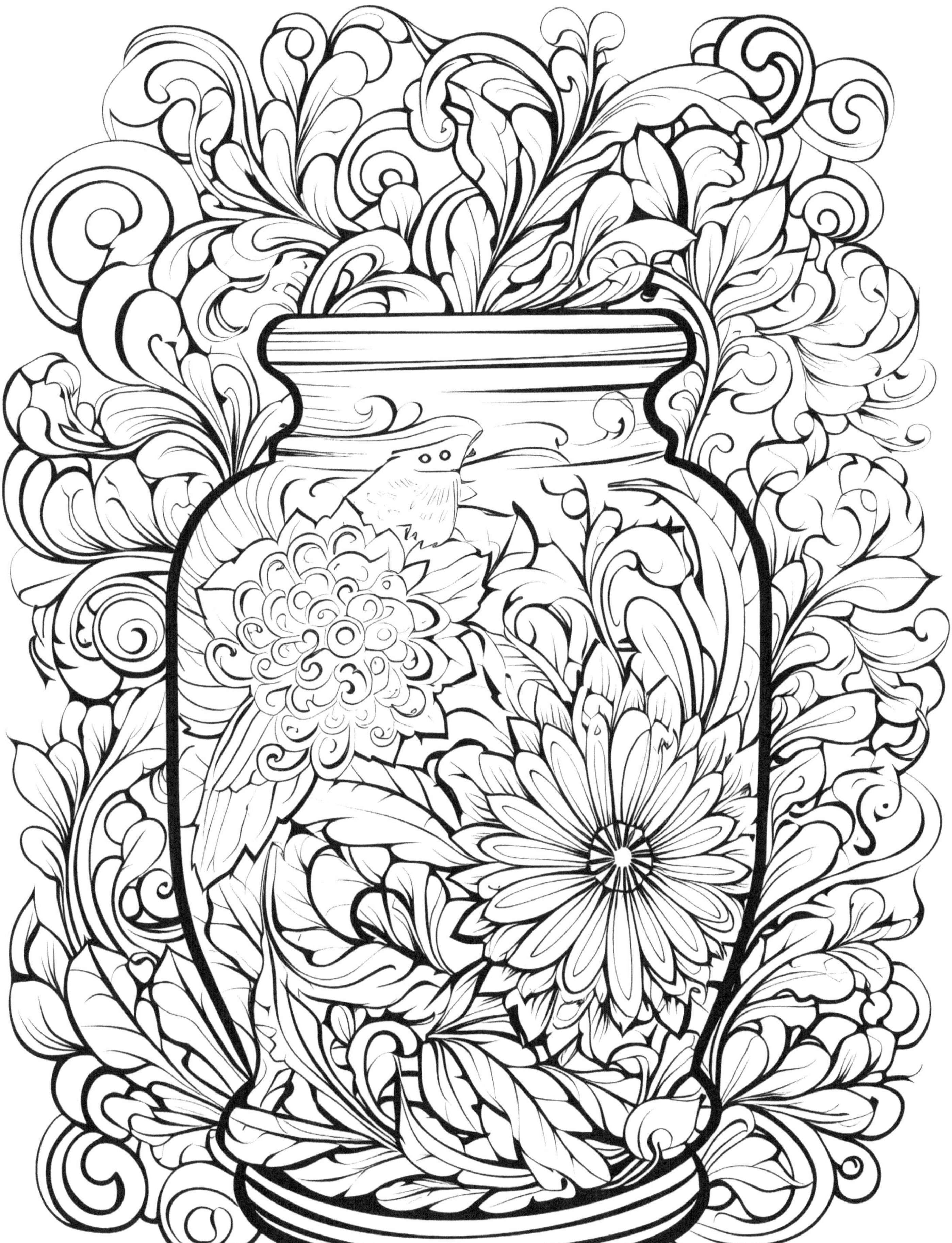

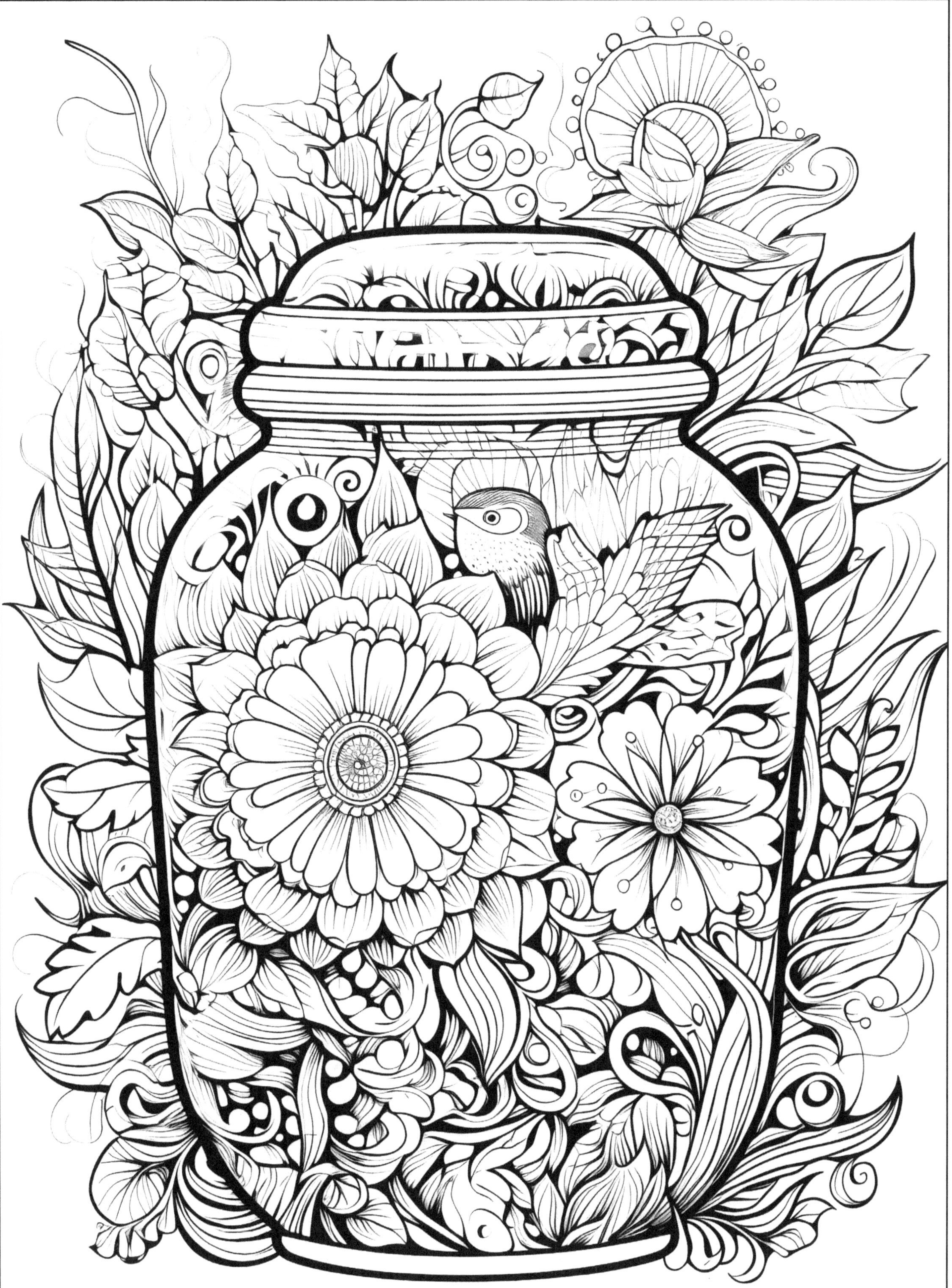

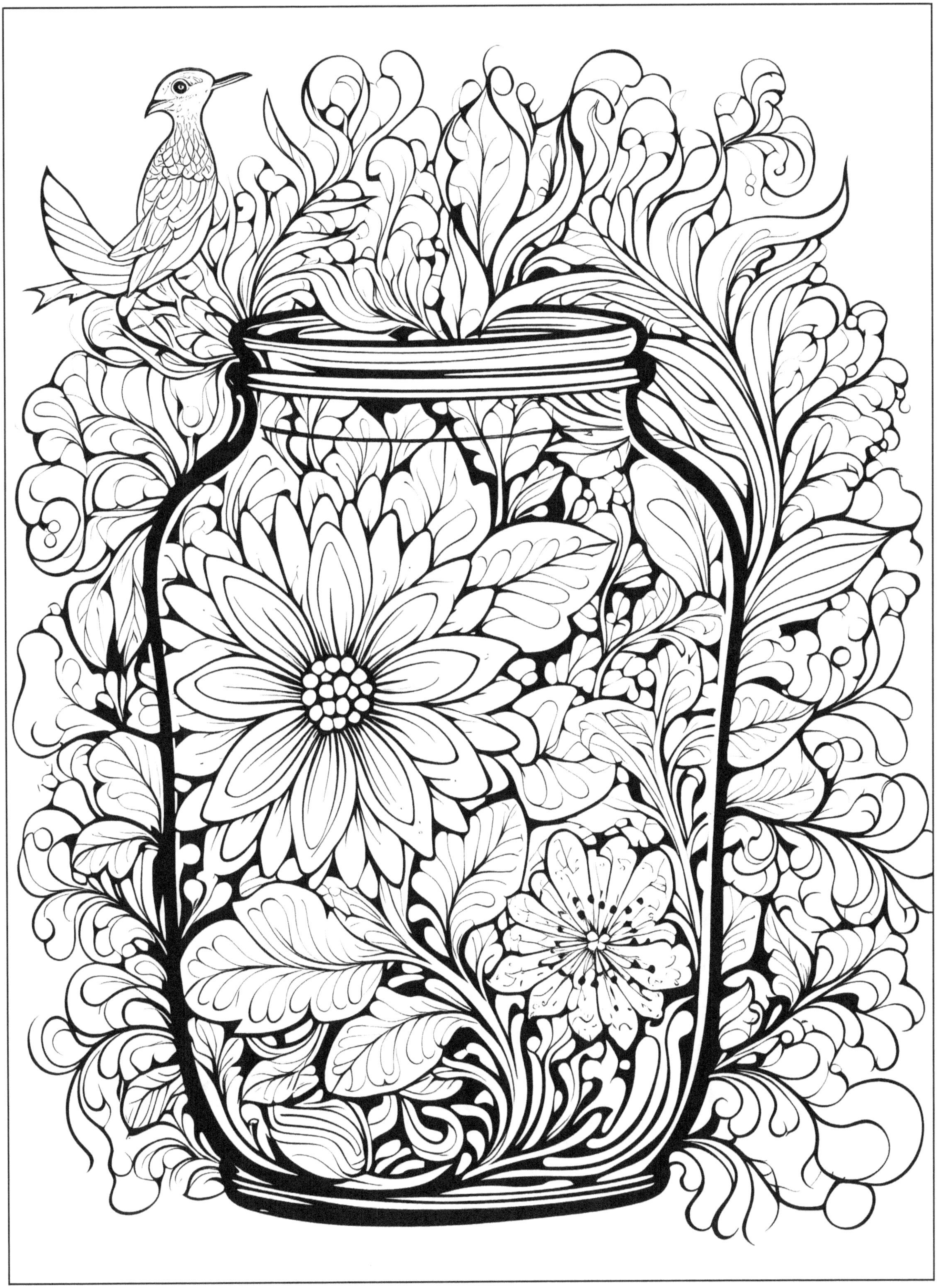

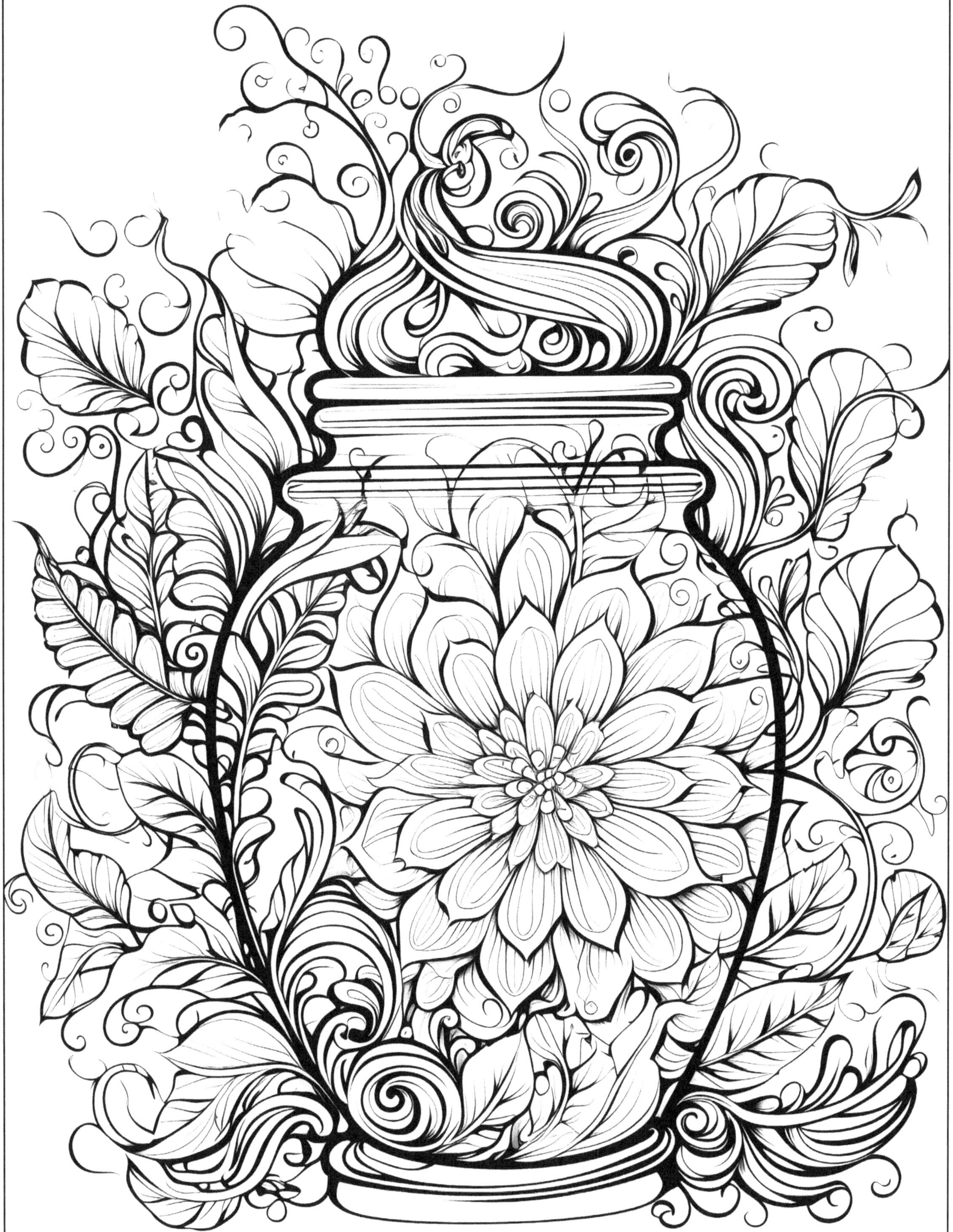

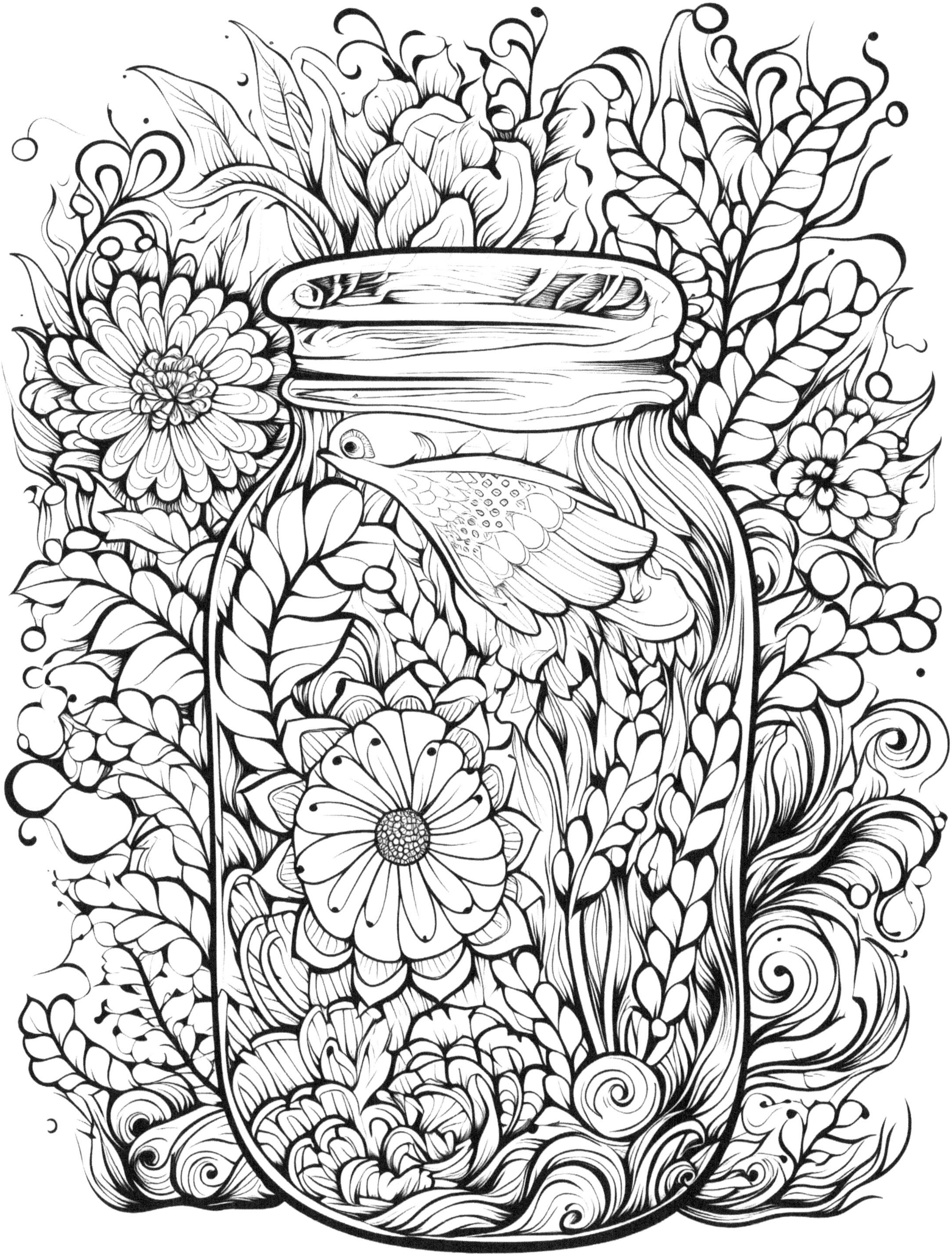

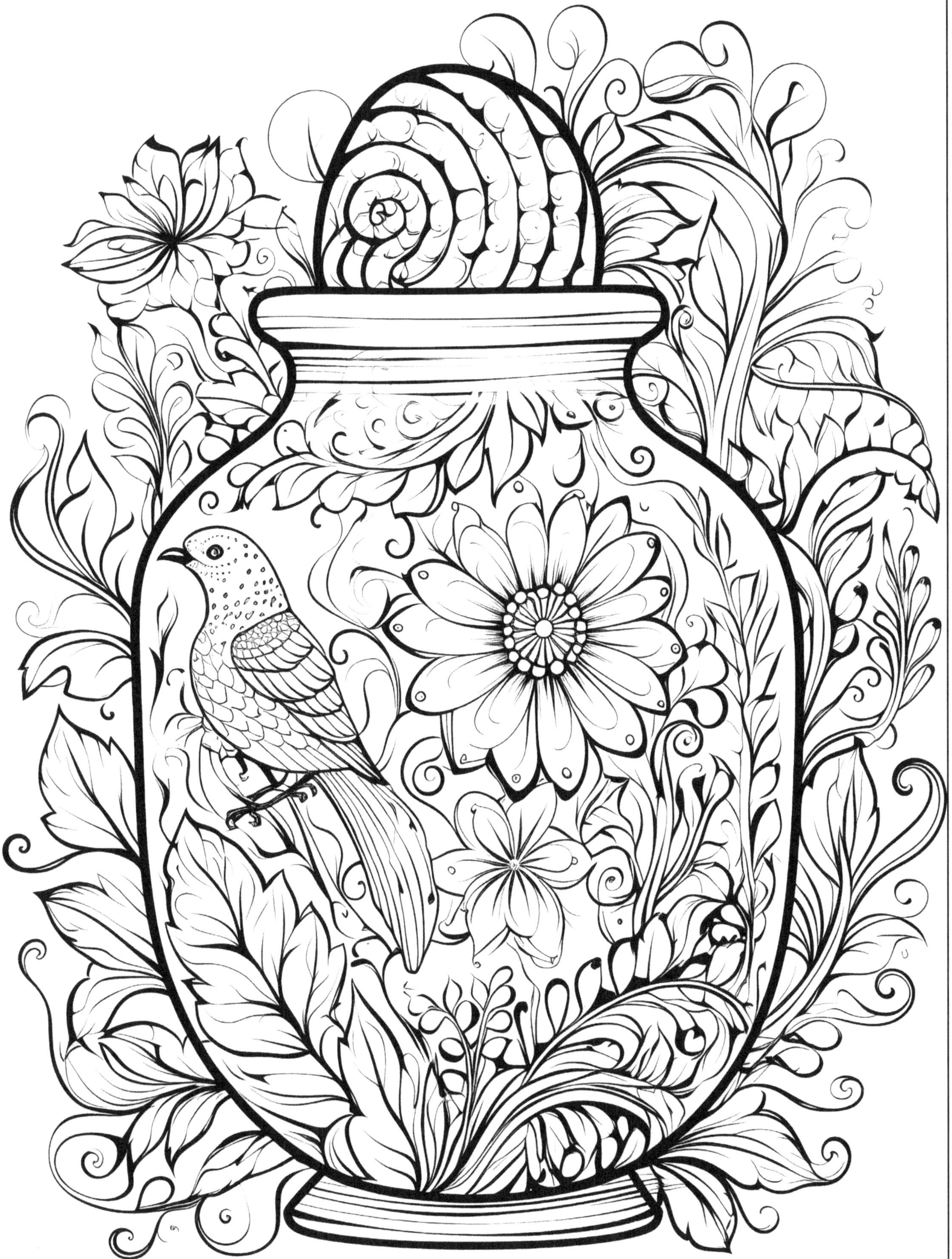

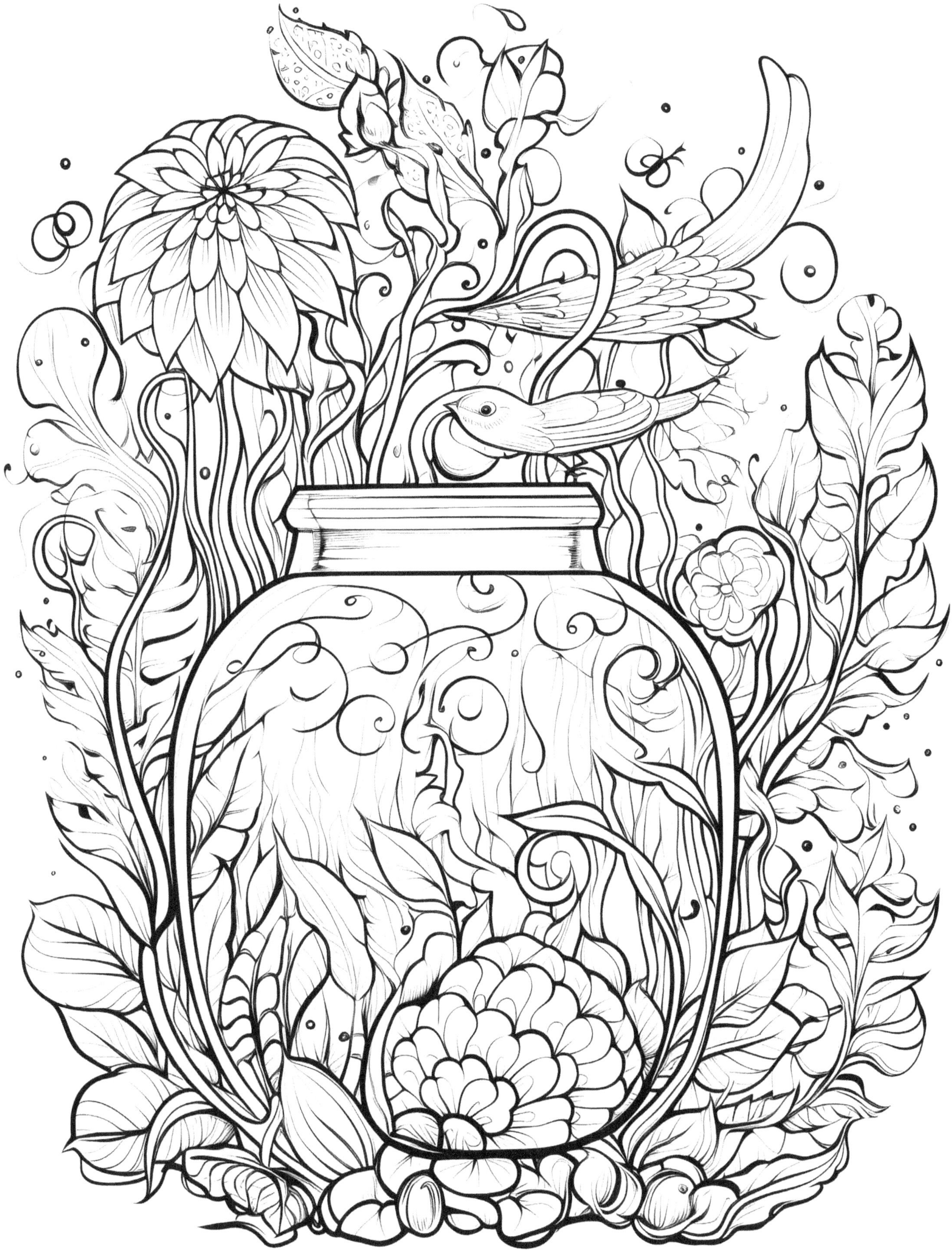

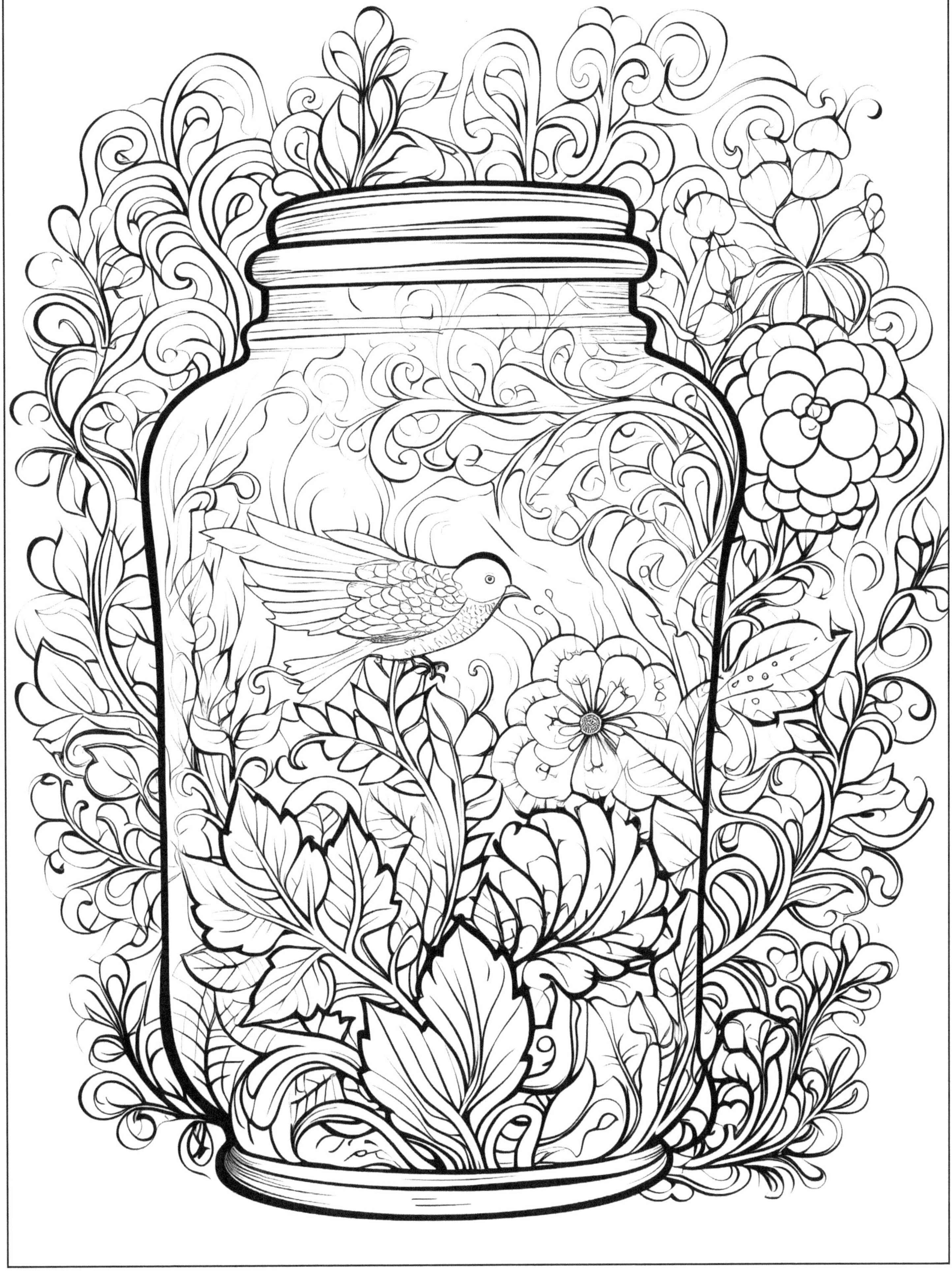

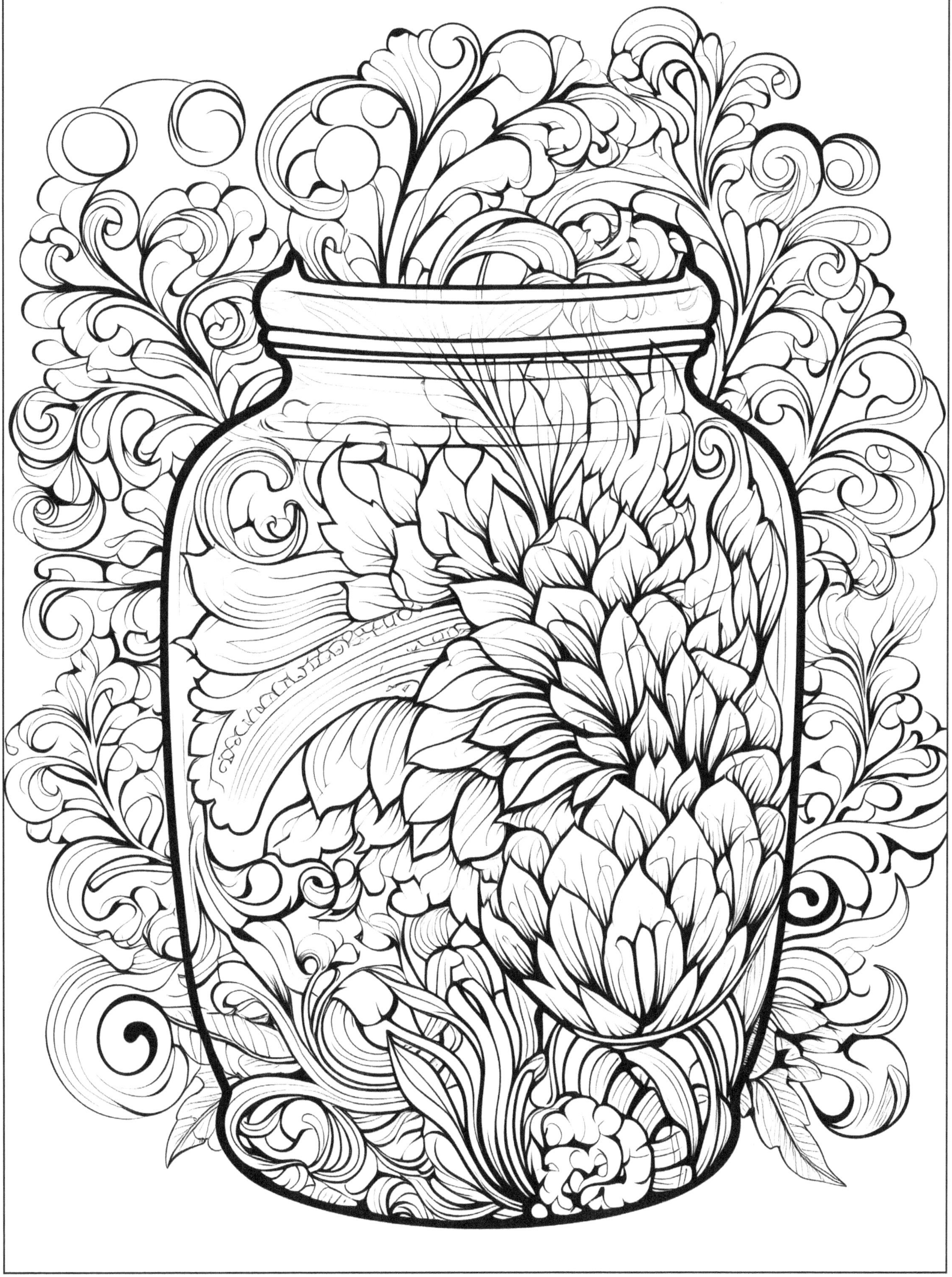

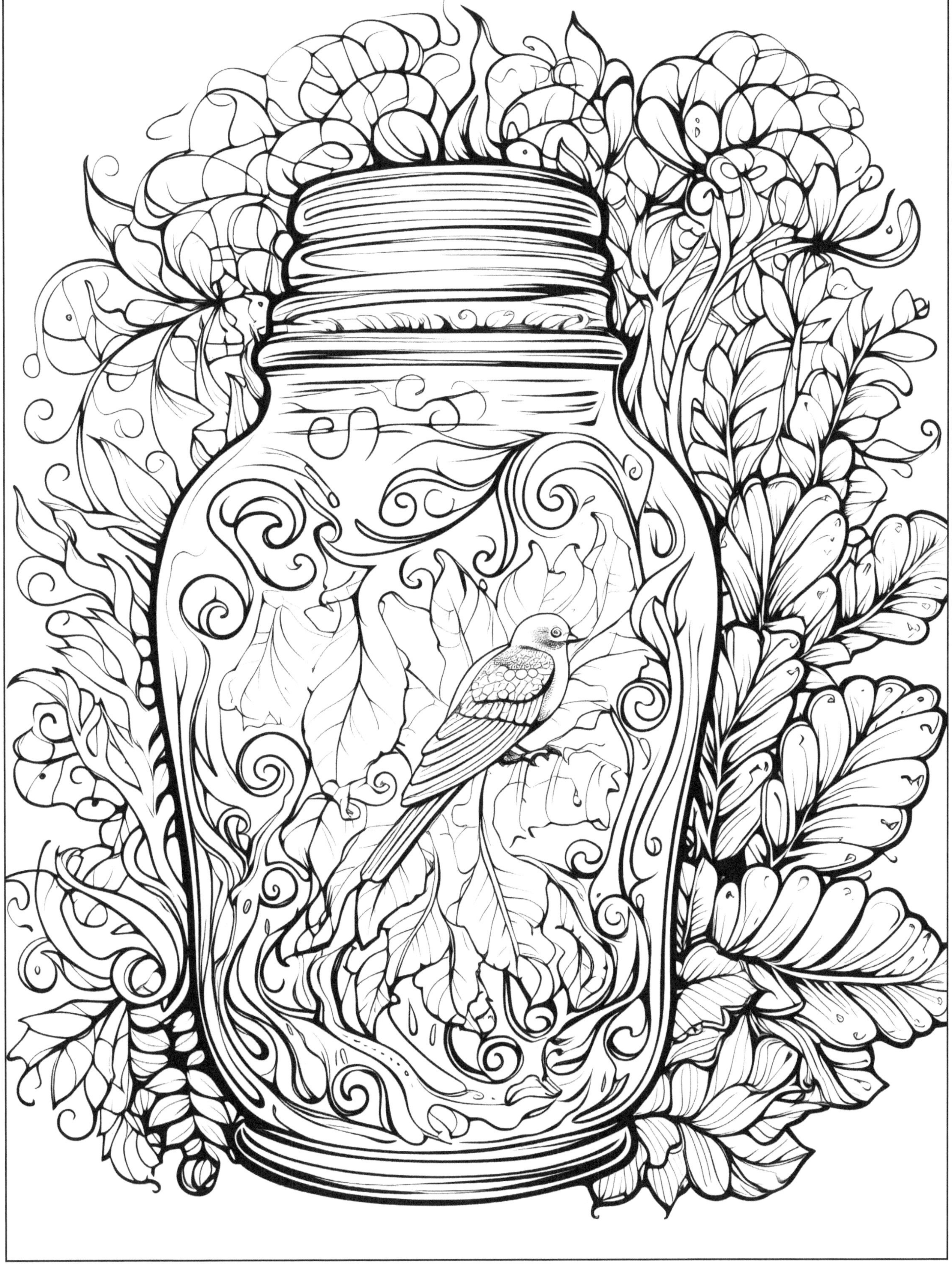

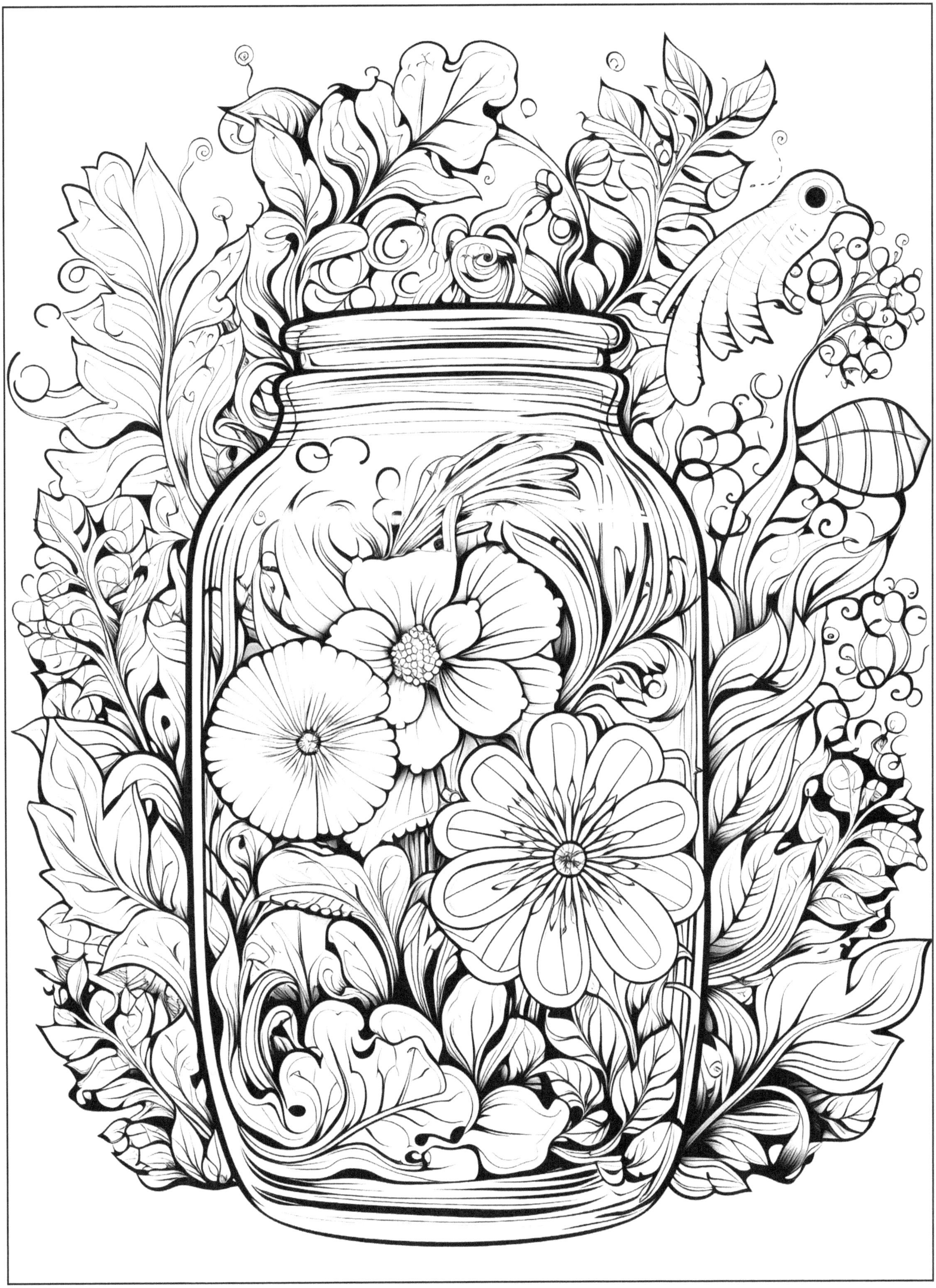

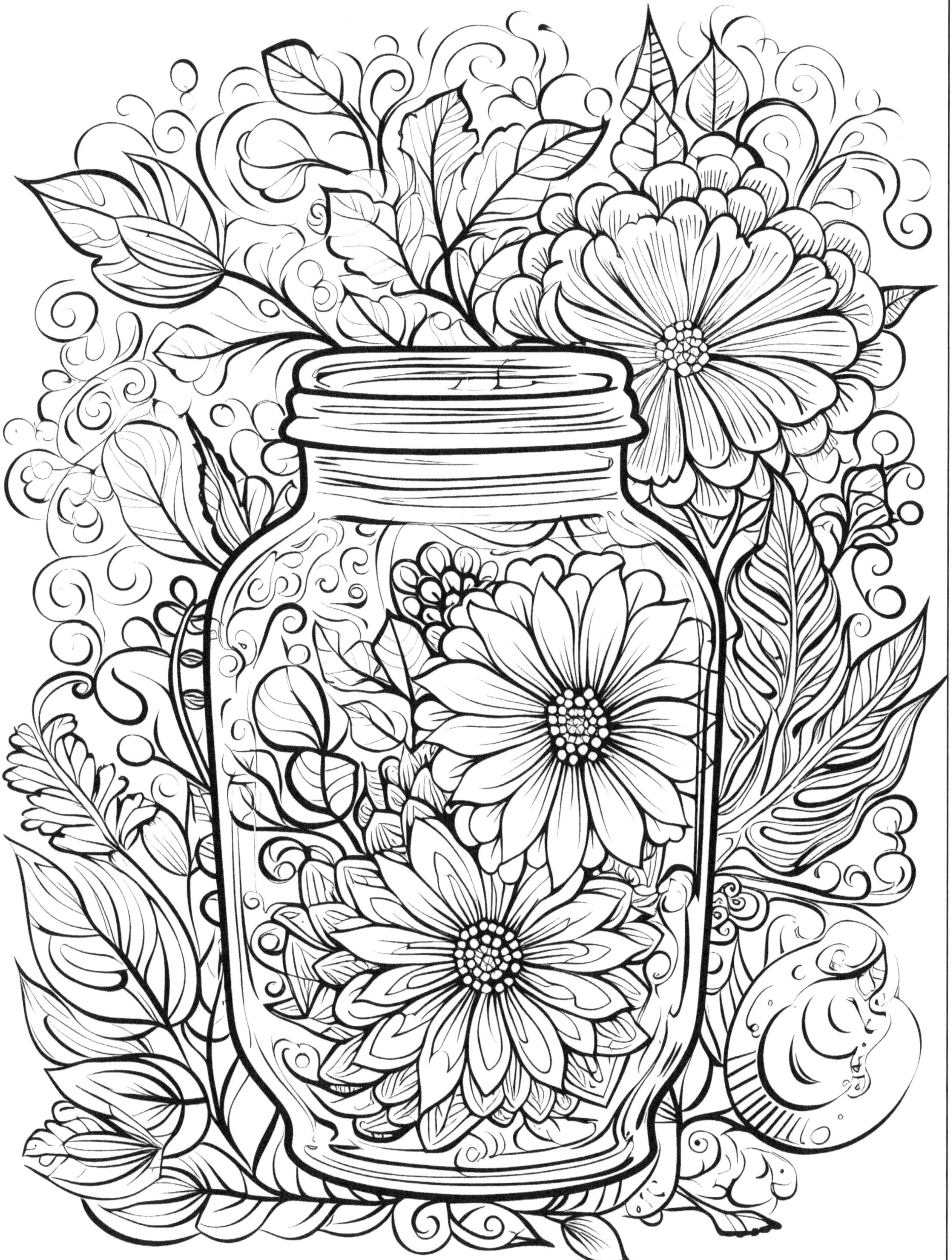

www.ingramcontent.com/pod-product-compliance
Lightning Source LLC
Chambersburg PA
CBHW082226290526
45794CB00009B/3688
9798859774876